S0-BDP-205

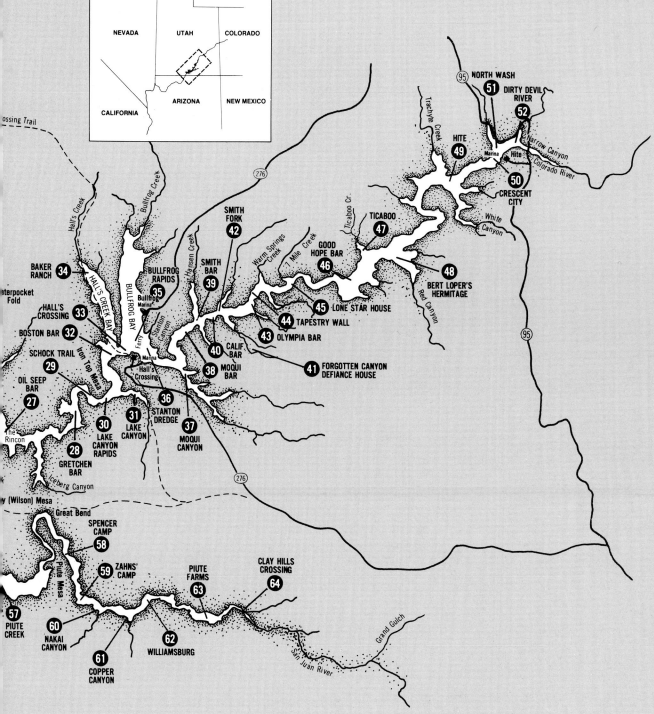

The above map and others in this book
are for orientation only and should not
be used for navigation. Glen Canyon
Recreation Area boundary not shown.

GHOSTS OF GLEN CANYON

History Beneath Lake Powell

C. GREGORY CRAMPTON

Cricket Productions
Salt Lake City, Utah

Copyright© 1986 by C. Gregory Crampton
Cover photograph and 16-page color photograph section, pages C-1 to C-16,
Copyright© 1994 by W.L. Rusho

All rights reserved. No portion of this book may be used or reproduced without written
permission from the publisher except in the case of brief quotations for review purposes.

REVISED

ISBN: 0-9630757-1-3

(Original edition published 1986 by Publishers Place, Ind., St. George, UT as
ISBN 0-939771-00-4)

Cover photographs by Will Rusho
Cover design by DataMax, Phoenix, AZ

CONTENTS

INTRODUCTION

Dr. Greg Crampton signs the register at the Kane Creek Boat Landing in Glen Canyon. June 24, 1958

WILL RUSHO

Glen Canyon was hot, but dazzling, on that June morning of 1958. Beneath the towering sandstone cliffs and monoliths, the sunlit brown waters of the Colorado River swirled majestically past the Kane Creek Boat Landing and on toward Crossing of the Fathers. As Public Affairs Officer for the Bureau of Reclamation, I was present at the boat landing to help erect a river bank sign advising boaters that, due to the construction of Glen Canyon Dam, they could proceed no farther by boat.

Pausing to look up the river, I saw a black object, apparently a rubber raft, floating in our direction. As it neared I made out two young men paddling energetically, while at the stern sat a man, obviously in charge, who seemed to be studying maps. When the raft slid onto the sandstone beach of the boat landing, the two younger men jumped out, erected a folding table, brought out food and drinks for lunch, set up a beach chair, and waited. Then the dark-haired man, wearing sun glasses, a Hawaiian-flowered shirt and a pith helmet, left the semi-comfort of his raft and strolled over to the chair. I could only conclude that this potentate, whoever he was, certainly knew how to enjoy his work.

When I walked up to introduce myself, he rose, put out his hand and said, "Hello. I'm Greg Crampton, Professor of History at the University of Utah." "Ah-ha!" I thought—an academic potentate!

Crampton then introduced me to the two assistants, actually graduate students, appropriately referred to as "slaves." He disclosed that he was just finishing his eighth research river trip down Glen Canyon, performed as his part of the University's contract with the National Park Service to make archaeological and historical studies of the canyon before it was inundated by Lake Powell. He said that during his trips he stopped to investigate anything that appeared to be constructed or altered by human beings, such as cabins, mining artifacts, or inscriptions on the rocks. He also said that in the intervals between trips he had obtained leads both from documentary research and from interviews with persons and women who had knowledge of historical events in Glen Canyon. From these leads he then visited specific locations on later rafting trips to search out artifacts and other evidence still visible on the ground.

I later learned that Greg had personally instigated the historical phase of the Glen Canyon study. Because of the abundance of prehistoric sites, National Park Service officials originally felt that only an archaeological study was needed. Greg wrote a persuasive letter to NPS officials that outlined the depth of history in the canyon and that urged them to authorize a separate historical study. Convinced that a better balance was needed, the NPS asked Crampton if he knew of a qualified historian who could undertake such a study. Needless to say, Greg took over the historical investigation, conducted from 1957 to 1963.

From our initial meeting by the river Greg and I eventually became close friends. His fascinating stories from Glen Canyon history spurred me to research past events myself, so that, over months and years, I became an avid student of local and regional history. Fortunately, for me as well as many others, Greg, as the guru of Colorado Plateau and canyonlands history, was always generous with his amazing wealth of knowledge. During succeeding years, Greg and I shared several historical endeavors. We were co-passengers on river trips down the San Juan and Colorado Rivers, we teamed up for trail research in three states, we gave lectures together, and we co-authored a paper and a book. On several campfire occasions, joined by our close mutual friend, Don Cecala, (and fortified by a large bottle of red wine), we indulged for hours in good-natured speculation about historic characters and events of the past.

Greg Crampton is unusual in that he writes not for fellow professional historians, but rather for the general public, in concise, clear terms, and with a judicious selection of stories and photographs that illuminate dramatic human encounters with Glen Canyon and with the Colorado River.

Greg would probably agree with author Ed Abbey who wrote that Glen Canyon was the heart of the red-rock country. Certainly Glen Canyon was at the

Ghosts of Glen Canyon

heart of Crampton's famous book *Standing Up Country*, (1964), and, I firmly believe, clearly at the heart of his entire career. Indeed, Glen Canyon, now submerged beneath the depths of Lake Powell, was the most visited, as well as the most historic canyon of the Colorado River. During its final few years of sunshine before inundation, with dam construction already underway, the canyon was at last visited by professional photographers and environmentalists. The Sierra Club later published a coffeetable book of photographs entitled, *The Place No One Knew*, a misnomer, for many people knew about Glen Canyon. What the title actually meant was that the Sierra Club leaders "didn't know."

I was one of those who did know, for I had five years of irregular exposure to Glen Canyon before it was submerged beneath the blue-green waters of Lake Powell. Then suddenly one day in early 1963, I realized that the canyon, as I knew it, as it had existed for millions of years, was disappearing fast under a shroud of rising water. Still, I failed to fully appreciate Glen Canyon until long after it had vanished.

To say that Glen Canyon was "lost" is probably incorrect; Glen Canyon was actually obliterated by the juggernaut of water development efforts then dominant in the American West. In the 1950's and early 1960's, along with millions of other western U.S. residents, I strongly supported the building of Glen Canyon Dam. Later, as part of my work for the Bureau of Reclamation, I conducted reporters and dignitaries to fascinating construction areas while explaining to them the valid reasons why the dam was needed. That the dam would eventually cause the flooding of Glen Canyon was a future development I thought little about.

After Glen Canyon Dam was completed, it took only a few years for Lake Powell to cover most of the better known scenic, archaeological, and historical sites in Glen Canyon. These tragic losses were partially obscured by the lake's own distinctive—and widely publicized—scenic beauty.

Yet we have paid an enormous price for Lake Powell. Before the lake was formed, Glen Canyon sustained a complete ecosystem that included plants, aquatic life, reptiles, mammals, and birds. Through it all, the Colorado River was moving, ever moving. One could hear the quiet slapping of water during the day. While lying in a sleeping bag, one could hear it in the night, the river murmuring softly, as if to declare "This river is alive!"

Glen Canyon also had depth, not only in the water, but in the convoluted cliffs that bordered the river. It had immense variety and color in the sandbars, the gravel bars, the side canyons, and the bright green "glens" of trees and bushes. To provide a glimpse of this scenic beauty, Greg Crampton and I have included in this book a 16-page sampling of color photographs that show portions of Glen Canyon as it was.

Most of the canyons of the Colorado River, before the advent of modern technology, were formidably inhospitable, the Grand Canyon awesomely so, but Glen Canyon never appeared so threatening. For almost two centuries, people came to Glen Canyon for a variety of reasons—exploration, cross country travel, scientific study, prospecting, sight-seeing, photography, or for the sheer fun of riding a rubber raft down the slow moving current. Whatever the reason, people saw in Glen Canyon a wilderness place they could enter without excessive danger. Of such places history is made.

If the politicians, the economic development promoters, the engineers—and even the general public—responsible for the dam had not had their way with Glen Canyon, probably the canyon someday would have been designated a National Park. For most families, friends, lovers, or Boy Scouts, boating down the canyon in an inexpensive rubber raft through magnificent scenery provided an easy, but unforgettable, adventure. Of course, the place was occasionally uncomfortable. It could be cold in winter, with ice in the river. During hot summer months, the rocky sandstone gorge often bore the brunt of brief wind storms sweeping across the desert. Generally, however, Glen Canyon was gentle, a delight to the men, women, and children who somehow learned of the canyon and were privileged to visit it.

Anyone who was fortunate enough to spend some time in Glen Canyon, before Lake Powell, would have to be considered a "ghost," myself included. Among the most prominent living ghosts of Glen Canyon would certainly be Greg Crampton himself, who knew the haunts and the stories of those long departed. Join with this "ghost" now as he delves into his extensive research to introduce you to an impressive panoply of other ghosts and illustrations from the past of Glen Canyon.

Will Rusho

PREFATORY NOTE

In this book I have told the Glen Canyon story with the armchair traveler and the Lake Powell visitor in mind. For me, the perfect travel experience requires a beautiful land and a land full of ghosts—beauty and history. Glen Canyon had both. Though altered, the beauty remains in Lake Powell. But it may not be apparent that most of the history—the ruins and remains, the sites and all of the visible traces of man's past—has been lost. The ghosts are under water.

To restore some measure of balance to our perception of Glen Canyon, I've prepared a short background essay. This is followed by a description and mini-history of some of the most interesting sites and places now covered by Lake Powell. Each site is illustrated with one or more photographs.

With the boating public in mind, I have keyed the sites to maps of the lake and I have numbered them in sequence from Glen Canyon Dam all the way up to Hite. The sequence is continued on the San Juan arm uplake to Clay Hills Crossing, and it is continued from Glen Canyon Dam down to Lee's Ferry. With this data and the photographs at hand, boaters may approximate on the lake the location of many of the sites.

The maps and photographs are for information, orientation, and planning, and should not be used for navigation. Some sites described herein are only partially covered by the lake. The approaches to such places by boat may vary with fluctuation of the lake level, and they may not appear exactly as shown in the photographic coverage. Caution is in order.

This book was done with the help of many people and I thank them all. Photos by a number of individuals, agencies, and institutions have lent dimension and perspective to the Glen Canyon story—a unique piece of Americana. Many of the things the photographers saw in the field from 1872 to 1963, and reproduced in these pages, won't be seen again. W.L. Rusho let me use many of his Glen Canyon photographs and draw upon his collections of Colorado River material. During the course of many hours on the lake, Don Cecala shared ideas about mapping Powell's underwater history.

—C.G.C.

BY *Will Rusho*

THE COLORFUL PAST OF GLEN CANYON

O f the past of Glen Canyon, the human drama was but one dimension, while the complex ecosystem, now submerged was another. Yet what most people remember from their visits was the kaleidoscope of warm colors reflecting from the sunlit cliffs, the shadowed alcoves, the brilliant green vegetation, and the sky flecked with white clouds. Regardless of logic, selective memory seems to show that *all* days in Glen Canyon were perfect!

The color photographs in this collection are but a sampling of Glen Canyon long ago. We have attempted to include enough photographs to suggest the variety of pattern and color in the main canyon, the side canyons, and in the quiet shaded grottos. Some archaeological or historical site photographs are included because these sites too comprised part of the scenic sweep of Glen Canyon.

We believe that every one of the sites shown in these photographs has been flooded or substantially affected by Lake Powell. While Rainbow Bridge has not been flooded, water from the lake completely fills the canyon just downstream from the Bridge and almost always backs into the channel beneath the bridge. Furthermore, the formerly lonely, magnificent solitude of this National Monument is regularly disturbed by crowds of tourists arriving from Lake Powell.

Several people have asked me to describe what Glen Canyon was "like" before Lake Powell. This difficult question could never be fully answered, since, for most people who came there, this colorful canyon, displaying thousands of ever-changing facets of light, shadow, and color, affected all aspects of experience, especially the deeply personal and subjective. Photographs, however magnificent, can illustrate but instants of time constrained

WILL RUSHO

The walls of Seven-mile Canyon tower over a hiker.

by the physical limitations of the camera. For those who unfortunately missed seeing Glen Canyon, the full emotional experience, and the memory derived from several days of camping, hiking, and photographing in this natural treasure, can only be imagined.

Petroglyphs near Hite, upper Glen Canyon, possibly of Fremont Culture.

(See p. 98)

C. GREGORY CRAMPTON

WILL RUSHO

Extensive panel of Anasazi petroglyphs at the mouth of Smith Fork is examined by Dr. Angus Woodbury of the University of Utah; (See p. 88)

C. GREGORY CRAMPTON

Wasp House in Lake Canyon; one of the many small Anasazi dwellings found in the Glen Canyon area.
(See p. 72)

"Moki" steps cut by Anasazi Indians to reach cave dwelling, now ruins, in Moqui Canyon.

(See p. 84)

C. GREGORY CRAMPTON

WILL RUSHO

Crossing of the Fathers, looking southwest. On November 7, 1776, the Dominguez-Escalante party; trying a desperate "short-cut" return to Santa Fe, cut steps for their horses to reach Padre Creek (bottom center), which they followed to the river. They waded and walked to the wide river bend at center where they crossed diagonally downstream. Their diary states "[We] finished crossing the river about five in the afternoon, praising God our Lord and firing off some muskets in demonstration of the great joy we all felt in having overcome so great a problem..." (See p. 30)

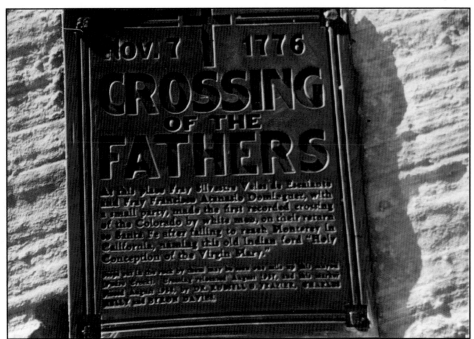

Plaque at the mouth of Padre Creek placed in 1938 by the Frazier-Kelly-Davies party.

WILL RUSHO

WILL RUSHO

Bert Loper's "Hermitage", where he lived while prospecting from 1909 to 1915, located on the left bank of the river near the mouth of Red Canyon.

(See p. 94)

Grave of Cass Hite, located near Hite's old cabin on Ticaboo Creek. Hite died in 1912.

(See p. 92)

WILL RUSHO

WILL RUSHO

Robert B. Stanton's famous gold dredge, built in 1901, lies rusting in the middle of the Colorado River.

(See pp. 80-83)

C5

A river traveler looks down on the Hite Ferry from a small Anasazi cliff ruin.

(See pp. 96-100)

WILL RUSHO

Steam boiler used by the Zahn brothers from 1902 to about 1915 overlooks the San Juan River.

(See p. 116)

WILL RUSHO

Hole-in-the-Rock, as seen from the Colorado River, where a treacherous 1000-foot descent was made by Mormon settlers, using 83 wagons, in January, 1880.

(See pp. 56-59)

WILL RUSHO

WILL RUSHO

WILL RUSHO

WILL RUSHO

WILL RUSHO

Music Temple, visited by the John Wesley Powell Expeditions of 1869 and 1871, where Powell recorded in his journal that "Old Shady" (Powell's brother, Walter) "sings us a song at night, [and] we are pleased to find that this hollow in the rock is filled with sweet sounds." Some of the expedition members chiseled their names into the soft sandstone wall. (See pp. 52-53)

Cathedral in the Desert, where overhanging walls seemed to shut out the world. A slowly dripping waterfall could be heard echoing softly through the chamber. It was located on Clear Creek, a short tributary of the Escalante River.

Two young
explorers
examine picto-
graphs in Davis
Gulch, a tribu-
tary of the
Escalante River.

Young hikers
enjoy the beauty
and the solitude
of Davis Gulch.

WILL RUSHO

WILL RUSHO

A family is dwarfed by the lofty walls of an alcove in Davis Gulch.

WILL RUSHO

*Sunshine
penetrates into
one of Glen
Canyon's steep-
walled side
canyons.*

WILL RUSHO

*A small side
canyon pool
mirrors the cliffs
and sky above.*

WILL RUSHO

Cataract Canyon, at the upper end of Lake Powell, contained about 40 miles of rapids. (See p.102)

A boating party pauses at the foot of Cataract Canyon in Mille Crag Bend.

A climber looks across the rolling slickrock toward the Colorado River and the mouth of Halls Creek. (See pp. 74-75)

Gathering clouds move over lower Glen Canyon.

A small rubber raft disturbs the tranquil surface of the Colorado River in upper Glen Canyon.

Buttes and cliffs at the mouth of Red Canyon in upper Glen Canyon. Note the distant boat on the river.

Aerial of the confluence of the San Juan River (bottom left) with the Colorado River, looking downstream.

Hall's Crossing, looking east across the Colorado River. Charles Hall operated a ferry here from 1881 to 1883.
(See pp. 74-75)

Gregory Natural Bridge on Fifty Mile Creek, a tributary of the Escalante River. (See p. 63)

WILL RUSHO

A hiker headed for Rainbow Bridge walks through the "Narrows" at the mouth of Bridge Canyon, where it joins Forbidden Canyon or Aztec Creek.

(See pp. 46-49)

C. GREGORY CRAMPTON

WILL RUSHO

As the sun lowers in the west, a hiker says farewell to lonely and magnificent Rainbow Bridge.

GLEN CANYON AND MAN

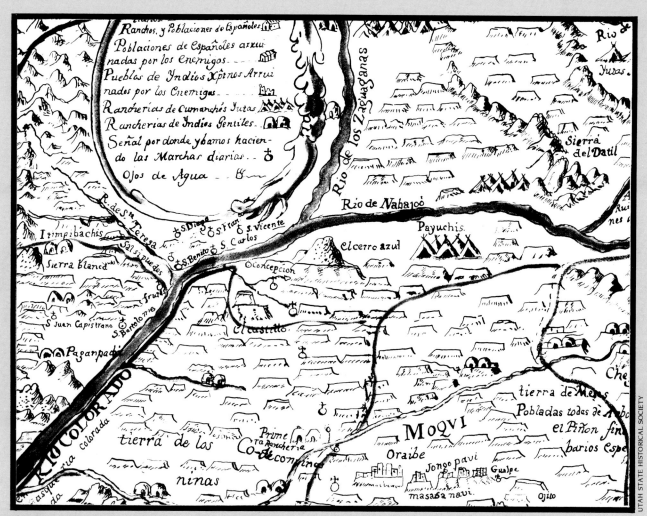

UTAH STATE HISTORICAL SOCIETY

The first portrayal of the Glen Canyon country. This is a section of a map drawn by Bernardo de Miera y Pacheco, cartographer of the Dominguez-Escalante expedition. The "Rio Colorado" is shown. The "R. de Sta. Teresa" is the Paria River. The "Rio de Nabajo" is the San Juan River. The "Rio de los Zaguaganas" is the Colorado River above the San Juan. "El Cerro Azul" is Navajo Mountain. The small circles with crosses are the several campsites of the expedition.

9

The First Canyon Dwellers

Prehistoric man, archeologists tell us, has been in the Southwest for a long time. For thousands of years the first people lived a simple life, hunting, foraging, and moving about a great deal. Gradually these early men developed more sophisticated ways of life and several interrelated cultures emerged, each showing a remarkable adaptation to the arid, resource-poor, rocky environment. One of these, the Anasazi culture, by the beginning of the Christian era, occupied the scenic Four Corners, a region extending outward from the common point where the boundaries of Utah, Colorado, New Mexico, and Arizona converge. The Anasazi (from the Navajo word meaning "ancient ones") claimed much of the Glen Canyon area. Another people, the Fremont (with close ties to the Anasazi in Glen Canyon), generally lived west and north of the Colorado River.

The Anasazi did some hunting, and they harvested a wide variety of wild plants, but life was chiefly supported by farming. They practiced irrigation, growing corn, beans, squash, and other crops. As farmers, these Indians became rooted to the soil. Housing gradually evolved from small, one-room pit dwellings, to hamlets and villages, to large apartment houses built of stone, adobe, and wood. The imposing ruins and remains of the great Anasazi urban centers, among them Mesa Verde National Park, Chaco Culture National Historical Park, and the national monuments at Aztec Ruins, Canyon De Chelly, Hovenweep, and Navajo are well known. Many lesser villages were built in open country and under recessed walls and cliffs in Glen Canyon.

The earliest Anasazi made baskets of high quality. The later people made fine pottery and a wide variety of tools and weapons. They developed art forms. They painted figures on rocks (pictographs) and pecked out others (petroglyphs). They used turquoise, shells, and feathers to make objects of adornment. Ceremonial life centered around the kiva, a circular chamber also used as a men's club room.

The Anasazi Indians favored upland areas where there was more rainfall and where resources were more plentiful, but during the 10th century A.D. more of them began to move down into Glen and San Juan canyons. This was a prehistoric frontier movement caused, perhaps, by swelling population and crowding in the more favored areas. In the canyon frontier people were scattered; communities were smaller and they were occupied for relatively brief periods. Maybe the canyon Anasazi were restless, or perhaps being frontiersmen they thought there might be something better in the next canyon. The canyons were no great barriers. The Indians forded the rivers and opened an amazing complex of trails.

During the 25 years before A.D. 1300 something happened. Perhaps there was a sustained drought or possibly it was the appearance of hostile nomads. Whatever the cause, the Anasazi pulled out of their homelands in Utah and Colorado and moved south to join the ancestors of the modern Pueblo Indians in Arizona and New Mexico. The great urban centers at Mesa Verde, Chaco, and the others were abandoned, becoming the first ghost towns in the Southwest now visited by thousands of people every year.

The history of the Fremont people parallels that of the Anasazi. They borrowed ideas from their neighbors, but they developed a culture of their own. They preferred hunting and gathering to farming. They found time to create many panels of well-executed and imposing petroglyphs and pictographs. Around A.D. 1300 they too left their homelands, emerging, perhaps, as one of the historic tribes living in the region today.

The prehistoric Indians of the Glen and San Juan canyons settled in the most desirable areas, namely, the canyon floors, and nearly all of their dwelling sites were covered by the rising waters of Lake Powell. In addition to the mainstream bottomlands, the Escalante River, Navajo Creek, and Moqui and Lake canyons (all Glen Canyon tributaries) were especially favored by the ancient ones.

One of the best of the Anasazi remains to escape the reservoir's rising waters is Defiance House in Forgotten Canyon a few miles uplake from the Bullfrog and Hall's Crossing marinas. This was a small village, or pueblo, consisting of dwelling areas, storage rooms, enclosed work areas, and a kiva. Painted in white on the wall above the structures are three, large, war-like human figures brandishing swords and holding circular shields. To archeologists investigating the site, these figures and the fortress-like location of the village suggested the name "Defiance House." Occupied for about 200 years, A.D. 1100-1300, the village has been restored and is easily accessible from the lake.

Two Utah State Historical Monuments some distance from Glen Canyon Recreation area incorporate partially restored Anasazi villages. Edge of the Cedars at Blanding, Utah, east of the recreation area, and Anasazi Indian Village, west of it at Boulder, Utah, were larger villages than any found in Glen Canyon. The settlement complex at Anasazi Village, built around A.D. 1075, deep inside Fremont territory, was abandoned in A.D. 1275. A museum with interpretive exhibits and displays will be found at each of these state monuments where the visitor may acquire some appreciation of the Anasazi culture which for so long dominated prehistoric life in the Glen Canyon region and much of the rest of the Southwest.

The history of the Glen Canyon region from A.D. 1300 until the coming of the Spaniards in 1776 is but dimly perceived. Peoples who lived mainly by hunting and foraging inhabited the lands of the ancient ones. The Ute Indians, whose domain included most of Colorado and much of Utah ranged over the northern Glen Canyon area. Their near relatives, the Southern Paiutes, also controlling a large territory, staked out the southern reaches. Some time after 1776 the Navajo Indians, moving westward, began to compete with the Paiutes, notably in the area east of the Colorado and south of the San Juan rivers, an area which in the course of time was added to the huge Navajo Indian reservation which now borders the southeastern section of the Glen Canyon National Recreation Area.

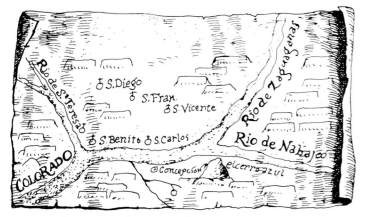

Spain and Mexico

The history of the Glen Canyon/Lake Powell region from about A.D. 1300 until the coming of the Spaniards is nearly blank, and that blank amounts to almost 500 years! By the time Dominguez and Escalante arrived in 1776, modern tribes had taken over some of the areas once occupied by prehistoric people. From the east the Ute Indians had edged into some of the upland areas. Their near relatives, known to anthropologists as Southern Paiutes, had taken a firm hold on the southern part of the Glen Canyon area on both sides of the Colorado River. Some time after 1776 the Navajo Indians began to compete with the Paiutes in the area east of the Colorado and south of the San Juan River.

The first white men to reach the upper basin of the Colorado River were Spaniards from New Mexico. The first to make a comprehensive traverse of the basin were two Franciscan friars, Francisco Atanasio Dominguez and Silvestre Velez de Escalante. The two Franciscans hoped to open a road between Santa Fe in New Mexico and Monterey in California and locate sites for missions and settlements en route. They did not get through. Owing to a late start they ran into bad weather and had to turn back. The exploration ended where it began, at Santa Fe.

Dominguez and Escalante and their companions traveled in a great circle through the four modern states of New Mexico, Colorado, Utah, and Arizona, most of the way through wilderness unknown to white men. Near Cedar City, Utah, they decided to head back to Santa Fe. Turning south, and then east near St. George, they traveled across the Arizona Strip. They were the first white men to reach the Colorado River where Lee's Ferry was established nearly a hundred years later. Unable to cross the river at that point, they worked their way upstream and found a ford later known as "El Vado de los Padres," in English translation, "The Crossing of the Fathers." Safely across on November 7, 1776, the explorers followed Indian trails and crossed the deep canyon of Navajo Creek to reach open country beyond.

Dominguez and Escalante were the discoverers of Glen Canyon, and the records they made are the earliest we have for much of the upper basin of the Colorado. The diary kept by Escalante, full as it is of geographical, ethnological, and biological information, and the beautiful charts made by Bernardo de Miera y Pacheco, expedition topographer, literally put the upper Colorado on the map.

During the revolutionary era that began in 1776, Spain was caught up in a swirl of international complications, and she sent no more official explorers to the canyon country. Soon she was plagued by revolution, and in 1821, Mexico emerged independent, to inherit all of Spain's vast dominions in North America.

There was little activity in Glen Canyon during the Mexican years, 1821-1848. The opening of a caravan trade between New Mexico and California was an important development. To launch their commerce, Antonio Armijo from New Mexico, with a trading party of 31 men, forded the Colorado at the Crossing of the Fathers and went on to California. He returned by the same route. The caravan trade lasted nearly 20 years.

Textiles from New Mexico were traded in California for mules and horses. Sometimes dozens of traders would form a caravan; on the return trip hundreds of animals would be driven along. This traffic was too heavy for the Glen Canyon crossing. An easier, longer route was soon discovered and called the Spanish Trail. It crossed the Colorado at Moab and the Green at Green River, thus heading the Glen Canyon barrier.

Traders on the Spanish Trail hurried along through the canyon country; American trappers stayed to look it over. The fur men, who would go anywhere after beaver, undoubtedly trapped the Glen Canyon region where the animals were plentiful, but the extent of this business is not well known since trappers kept meager records. Denis Julien, a trapper of French descent, left his name and the date, 1836, on a cliff in Cataract Canyon, which suggest that the fur men were working the canyons in boats. By the time the region passed to the United States, through the Mexican cession of 1848, the great years of the Rocky Mountain fur trade had ended and quiet days had settled on the canyons for a time.

Mormon Frontier

On November 6, 1858, 82 years almost to the day after Dominguez and Escalante passed this way, Jacob Hamblin and ten companions forded the Colorado at the Crossing of the Fathers. They were en route to villages of the Hopi Indians where they planned to do some missionary work for the Church of Jesus Christ of Latter-day Saints. A pioneer in the settlement of Utah's "Dixie," Hamblin, as missionary, Indian agent, pathfinder, peacemaker, and colonizer, was a central figure in the Glen Canyon country for over 20 years. He seems to have spent half of his life on horseback. He crossed the Colorado many times at El Vado and at Lee's Ferry. In the fall of 1860, on his third missionary trip to the Hopis, Hamblin ran into some hostile Navajos. One of the party, George Albert Smith Jr., was killed by them.

Young Smith was the first casualty in a serious ten-year struggle between the Mormons and the Navajo Indians. It grew

out of a clash of frontiers in the canyon lands. Moving eastward from their base settlements along the Virgin River, the Mormons met Navajos in the canyons east of the Colorado. Since 1846-1848, when American replaced Mexican rule in New Mexico, the Navajos had been troublesome. As their raids and attacks on the settlements increased, military forays were sent against them. Finally, in 1863 and 1864, most of the Navajos gave in to American forces and were sent into exile at Fort Sumner in eastern New Mexico. Most, but not all. Many fled to the canyon country and from there began raiding the Mormon settlements west of the river. At times the Navajos found the Paiutes ready allies.

When the Navajos stepped up their raids, open warfare broke out between the two peoples. Moving rapidly, the Indians crossed the river, rounded up stock in the Mormon settlements, and drove them across the river at the Crossing of the Fathers. More than once the Utah militia chased the marauding Navajos to the crossing without catching them. The war dragged on. Lives were lost. Finally, in 1870, at Fort Defiance, Jacob Hamblin and John Wesley Powell worked out a peace treaty between the Navajos and the Mormons.

Trade sprang up after the war. On his second trip through the canyons of the Colorado, Powell arrived at the Crossing of the Fathers the first week in October, 1871. While camped near there, the first Navajo trading party splashed across the river en route to the Mormon settlements. Thus began a peaceful commerce that lasted, with some near interruptions, for many years.

One of the first to engage in the Indian trade was John D. Lee who, late in 1871, moved to the mouth of the Paria River, 40 miles downstream from the Crossing of the Fathers. The place was isolated, remote. Stalwart Emma Lee called it "Lonely Dell." Later arrivals called it "Lee's Ferry." For some time Brigham Young, the "Colonizer President" of the Mormon Church, had planned for the settlement of the valley of the Little Colorado River. A move in that direction would require a ferry at the mouth of the Paria, the only feasible crossing place for wagons. Now that the Indians were at peace, the time was right. John D. Lee, under a cloud for complicity in the Mountain Meadows Massacre, was sent by the church to get things started. He did engage in Indian trade but that was incidental to the main business of opening a ferry. Although he was present when formal ferry service was begun in January, 1873, Lee spent little time at the place later named for him. Colonization of the Little Colorado followed during the 1870s, and the church operated Lee's Ferry as a link and a bond between the older settlements in Utah and the newer ones on the Arizona frontier. Once the new colonies seemed well established and stable, the church, in 1909, sold the ferry. For some of the details of Lee's Ferry's varied history from the Spanish *entrada* to the present, see No. 66.

In another direction, the Mormon Church, in 1879, organized a formal mission to colonize the open country along the San Juan River above the canyon lands. A scouting party crossed the Colorado River at Lee's Ferry and traveled north through the Navajo country to the San Juan River where a suitable place for a settlement was found. The scouts then returned by an easy route which took them north to Moab and the Spanish Trail, which they followed back to the starting point near Cedar City in south central Utah. A large colonizing mission was formed, but rather than journey to the San Juan by either the Spanish Trail or by the somewhat more difficult route by Lee's Ferry and the Navajo country, the leaders of the expedition decided to cut directly "across lots" where there was no road, not even a trail. The trek across Glen Canyon at Hole-in-the-Rock and through the "impassable" region beyond the Colorado River is one of the remarkable and heroic achievements in Western history. The pioneer band expected to spend six weeks en route to their destination on the San Juan River. They spent six months instead. For details about the crossing of Glen Canyon see No. 24 and No. 33, Hall's Crossing.

Powell and the Colorado

In 1857 Lt. G.K. Warren, of the Army's Corps of Topographical Engineers, finished a large map of the trans-Mississippi West that incorporated the most reliable data taken from reports of Western exploration issued over the preceding 50 years. On his map, published by Congress in 1859, Lt. Warren was careful to represent only those areas which had actually been explored. Other areas were marked "unexplored." One of the largest unexplored blanks was the canyon wilderness of the Colorado River. To the one-armed Civil War veteran, Major John Wesley Powell, the Colorado was a challenge. The river and the canyons were a mystery. Powell planned to fill in the blanks on the map, to tackle the "Great Unknown," as he termed it. The canyons would be a book of

"revelations" about the geological nature of earth's crust, and he wanted to read the book.

The story of Powell's two voyages of discovery through the long line of canyons below Green River, Wyoming is the best-known chapter in the history of the Colorado River. With four boats and ten men aboard, Powell began the first trip on May 24, 1869. On July 28, after taking a pounding in the rapids of Cataract Canyon, they reached the Dirty Devil at the head of Glen Canyon. It was easy going now. the explorers rested on their oars and enjoyed the scenery. They spent two memorable, restful days at Music Temple just below the mouth of the San Juan River. It was the cool, shady side canyons, so welcome to the travelers, that Powell remembered when he gave the name "Glen" to the magnificent canyon between the Dirty Devil and the Paria rivers.

Below the Paria the voyagers entered the Grand Canyon. After 26 days of grueling travel they made it through Grand Canyon and came out to the open country at the mouth of the Virgin River. Of the ten men who had started the journey, six completed it. The brothers O.G. and Seneca Howland, and William Dunn quit the expedition at Separation Rapids in Grand Canyon. While walking out to the settlements, all three were killed by Shivwits Indians.

The second Powell voyage, 1871-1872, funded by Congress, largely duplicated the first, but it was better organized for the collection of information. Leaving Green River May 22, 1871, the expedition reached Glen Canyon on September 30. A week later the explorers arrived at the Crossing of the Fathers (Powell used the term "El Vado de los Padres") where supplies had been left for them by the Mormon scout Jacob Hamblin. At the Paria River Powell ended the river exploration for 1871. He spent the rest of the year and the first months of 1872 surveying and mapping in southern Utah and the Arizona

Strip. The river trip was resumed in August of 1872 but was discontinued at the mouth of Kanab Canyon.

Although the voyages were certainly adventurous, Powell's interest was in scientific discovery. During the voyages he saw everything. He steered the first expedition through a thousand miles of the canyons of the Colorado; he climbed out to the rims to study the country; he made geological sections and observed the stars at night; he studied Indian ruins; he appreciated the grandeur of the landscape all the way; he demonstrated that the river in the canyons was navigable; he put names on the map; he formulated geological theories later developed in important books.

The year 1871 marks the beginning of the Powell Survey, making him one with King, Hayden, and Wheeler who were at work making elaborate studies and surveys in the American West. Powell worked with the Smithsonian Institution until 1874 when his survey was transferred to the Department of the Interior and officially named the United States Geographical and Geological Survey of the Rocky Mountain Region. Powell and a roster of highly competent men mapped and studied a large part of the Colorado Plateau and published their findings in books of lasting value. Powell wrote on the river explorations and the physical features of the valley of the Colorado (1875), on the Uinta Mountains (1876), and on the arid lands of the United States with particular reference to the lands of Utah (1879). G.K. Gilbert wrote about the Henry Mountains (1877). C.E. Dutton wrote about the high plateaus of Utah (1880) and the Grand Canyon (1882).

John Wesley Powell had conquered the "Great Unknown" and he had very nearly filled in that big blank left on the map by Lt. G.K. Warren. Powell went on to a distinguished career in government science. He was named the second director of the U.S. Geological Survey, and in a concurrent position, he served as director of the Bureau of American Ethnology, a division of the Smithsonian Institution. At the time of his death in 1902 Major Powell was honored for his contributions to Western exploration, geology, anthropology, reclamation, and conservation. Many of the ideas he developed in the promotion of government science were generated during those two river trips down the Colorado.

The Wheeler survey, mentioned above, was officially called the U.S. Geographical Survey West of the Hundredth Meridian. It was directed by George M. Wheeler, U.S. Army, and overlapped somewhat the work of the Powell Survey in the Glen Canyon region, and there is some confusion in the names on the maps of the two surveys.

Gold Rush

In March, 1880, Indians killed two prospectors in Monument Valley. James Merrick and Ernest Mitchell had been looking for a hidden mine thought to be the source of silver used by Navajo Indians in making their jewelry. When a search party found samples of silver ore with the bodies, it was believed the prospectors had found the hidden mine, although no one after them ever found out where the silver samples came from. The Merrick-Mitchell "mine" was a lodestone for prospectors who searched for it in the Monument Valley/Navajo Mountain region for at least 25 years. Among the searchers was Cass Hite, a prospector from Colorado. Hite struck up a friendship with the Navajo Chief Hoskininni who told him gold could be found in Glen Canyon. Following the chief's directions Hite went to the place later named after him and soon discovered placer gold on both sides of the Colorado where there was a good crossing—a "dandy crossing," Hite called it. This was in September, 1883.

For a time the prospector had the canyon to himself. It was quiet, uninhabited. Quite probably the only other resident above Lee's Ferry was Charles Hall whose ferry business at Hall's Crossing had all but vanished.

Suddenly, the quiet days were gone. As Hite's gold discoveries became known, a light rush of prospectors began.

"Hite," on the Colorado at Dandy Crossing, was the first focus of interest. Here a mining district was organized in 1885; a post office and store were opened in 1889. As new discoveries were made, momentum increased. Prospectors rushed by the hundreds to prospect in what must have been the most difficult mining region any of them had ever seen. They entered the canyon at Hite or Hall's Crossing, even Hole-in-the-Rock and Lee's Ferry, and they found gold all along the Colorado from the Dirty Devil to Lee's Ferry. Extremely fine gold it was—gold dust literally—and very difficult to recover by any method of placer mining. The most productive locations were the gravel terraces, in some places rising up to 200 feet above the river. These were Ice Age gravels washed into the canyon by the heavy runoff from melting glaciers.

Mining in Glen Canyon was no easy matter. Water for mining was right at hand but the silty river quickly wore out pumping machinery. Supply points were distant; roads were poor, and getting about was difficult. You could boat down the river to the claim. Then what? Although the river flowed quietly with only a few riffles, to row upstream very far was out of the question. The miners developed trails leading into and out of the canyon, rivaling those created centuries earlier by prehistoric Indians. Indeed, in some places the miners picked out trails suitable for pack animals right over foot trails pecked out by the Anasazis. Practically no gold was found in Glen's tributary canyons, although they were prospected along with the nearby Navajo Mountain and Henry Mountains.

In 1892 gold was discovered in the canyon of the San Juan River, and a rush bent itself in that direction. The best diggings were found between Clay Hills Crossing and the Great Bend, where extensive gravel deposits were intensively prospected. Several mining districts had been organized by 1895. The diggings on the San Juan were easier to reach than those in Glen Canyon, and in some places heavy machinery was installed in attempts to recover the elusive, powdery gold.

Within 12 years after the turn of the century, the gold fever in Glen and San Juan canyons had subsided. There were some later mining activities—copper, petroleum, and in recent times, uranium—but these touched the canyons only slightly. There was a revival of gold mining during the Great Depression, but it did not compare with the boom times, 1883-1912.

The Engineer and The Promoter

The Glen Canyon gold rush had some bearing on the formation of the Denver, Colorado Canyon and Pacific Railroad, organized by Frank M. Brown. The firm planned to build a railroad from Grand Junction, Colorado, to the Pacific through the canyons of the Colorado. Brown engaged Robert Brewster Stanton, a prominent engineer, to make a survey for the line. Starting at Green River, Utah, in May, 1889, Stanton reached Dandy Crossing and Hite on June 24th after a rough trip through Cataract Canyon. After passing through Glen Canyon, the survey party met disaster when President Brown and two others drowned in the rapids of Marble Canyon. Before the end of the year Stanton returned and, with better equipment, resumed the survey. Starting at the mouth of North Wash, he carried the railroad survey through Grand Canyon and on to the Gulf of California.

The railroad was not built. Stanton argued the feasibility of the line from an engineering standpoint, but capital was more timid than the doughty engineer. However, Robert B. Stanton had seen enough of Glen Canyon to convince him that a fortune was to made there in gold mining. Within a few years he was back to test his conviction.

The most elaborate mining operation in Glen Canyon during the gold rush was undertaken by the Hoskaninni Company, the brainchild of Robert B. Stanton. The engineer seems to have looked upon Glen Canyon as a gigantic natural sluice box, its bed lined with gold. To recover the metal he would use a big floating dredge, commonly seen in the western United States at that time. If a pilot machine worked well, he would install several of them in the canyon. He would build dams in tributary canyons—and even on the Colorado—to generate power to operate the dredges. He would stake out and claim the entire canyon from the Dirty Devil to Lee's Ferry. If the claims were contiguous, then the assessment work required by law for each claim could be done on one or several claims. Stanton liked to think big. For the millions he believed the river held in its sands, he would dredge Glen Canyon, a distance of 170 miles.

Capitalists liked his ideas. Tests made by Stanton in Glen Canyon measured up to expectations. Appointed superintendent of field operations, Stanton went to work. Crews were sent to separate points to build roads and improve trails in preparation for the installation of several dredges. One crew went to the river at Hole-in-the-Rock, and by cutting steps in the Mormon road, just 20 years old, made it safer for use by pack animals. By the end of 1899 the entire canyon had been staked and 145 claims had been recorded.

Meanwhile, a dredge, shipped in parts to the railhead at Green River, was hauled to the river and assembled at Camp Stone, a site two and a half miles above the mouth of Bullfrog Creek. The huge machine was put in operation in the spring of 1901. It was a failure. The fine gold dust simply floated over the amalgamators and back to the river. Stanton had proved that large-scale mechanized mining in Glen Canyon didn't work. The one man-powered shovel, sluice box, and pan seemed to be the best bet. For details on the assembly and operation of the dredge see No. 36.

Stanton's lesson about large-scale mining was lost on Charles H. Spencer who also liked to think big. Boldly imaginative, he managed to find investment capital to support elaborate mining schemes in San Juan and Glen canyons which, merely to list them, leave one breathless. On the San Juan he attempted to extract gold from the Wingate sandstone. Building a road to bring in heavy machinery, Spencer set up a crusher and amalgamator at the river's edge. There was some gold in the "ore" but not enough to pay costs.

Next scene: Lee's Ferry. If, as Stanton had believed, Glen Canyon was a gold-lined sluice box, then Spencer reasoned Lee's Ferry at the foot of the canyon ought to be a good place to strike it rich. Moreover, at Lee's Ferry there was a broad outcropping of the soft Chinle shale which Spencer had already determined carried more gold than the Wingate. He started off with a pneumatic pipe dredge which forced river and sand up through a casing to the amalgamating tables. Then he activated a hydraulic operation which pumped water through high-pressure nozzles and washed the Chinle down through flumes and sluices.

To power the machinery Spencer needed coal to generate steam. A good coal prospect was found on a branch of Warm Creek, a Glen Canyon tributary 28 miles upstream from the ferry. To reach the mine Spencer's men built an unbelievable trail up over the Echo Cliffs towering 1,500 feet directly above Lee's Ferry. However, rather than use the trail to haul coal by mule train, Spencer decided to ship it down to the ferry by boat, whereupon a huge 92-foot-long steamer, bought in San Francisco, was assembled at the mouth of Warm Creek. Coal from the mine was brought down to a storage yard and operations center at the head of Warm Creek Canyon, hauled in wagons down to the mouth of the canyon, and loaded on the "Charles H. Spencer," the largest boat ever to operate in Glen Canyon.

All of this activity took place in less than three years, 1909-1912. Approaching these schemes with boundless energy and considerable sums of other people's money, Spencer finally had to admit failure and shut down operations. Everything had gone wrong. On the San Juan the Wingate "ore" was impossibly low grade. At Lee's Ferry the pipe dredge ran into bedrock; the Chinle shale gummed up the sluice boxes and amalgamating tables. In the spring of 1912 the "Charles H. Spencer" was put in service, but by then it had become apparent that the Lee's Ferry project was doomed. In any event the "Spencer" would not have helped much. It turned out that the boat used up almost all the coal it could carry to make the 28-mile run back upstream to Warm Creek. After five one-way trips the boat was tied up and never used again.

Spencer's gold mining operation at Lee's Ferry was the last of any size in Glen or San Juan canyons. The gold rush, 1883-1912, unique in American history owing to the canyon locale, was over. Within a few years the once busy placer diggings—Hite, Ticaboo, California Bar, Gretchen Bar, Klondike Bar, Williamsburg, and the others—were ghost camps on the Colorado and the San Juan. Excepting Lee's Ferry, the entire gold mining area in both Glen and San Juan canyons has been inundated by Lake Powell.

Raising the Ghosts

As the gold rush waned, tourists began to appear in the canyons. In 1902, F.S. Dellenbaugh published his *Romance of the Colorado River,* a well-illustrated history covering the centuries from the time of the Spanish discoveries to the Stanton railroad survey. Then in 1908, he brought out *Canyon Voyage,* the first satisfactory account of the second Powell expedition, of which he was a member. Both books did much to stimulate recreational travel on the river. Now men came to see the canyons, not to see what they could get out of them. In 1909, Julius Stone, Stanton's associate in the Hoskaninni venture, with Nathaniel Galloway at the helm, boated through the canyons from Green River, Wyoming, to Needles, California, just for adventure. In 1911, Ellsworth and Emery Kolb, photographers at Grand Canyon, left Green River, Wyoming, on a photographic tour using Dellenbaugh's *Canyon Voyage* as a

guide. En route they made the first significant motion pictures of the canyons. Ellsworth's book, *Through the Grand Canyon from Wyoming to Mexico,* (1914, and many reprintings) was further stimulus to canyon travel. After World War I, David E. Rust, who had been in the gold rush, began running commercial tours in Glen Canyon using folding boats. But interest in Glen Canyon boating developed slowly. Most of the early canyon country tourists headed overland for Natural Bridges or Rainbow Bridge. The early scientific expeditions generally relied on horses.

In 1921, the U.S. Geological Survey and the Southern California Edison Company undertook the mapping of the Colorado River from the head of Cataract Canyon through Narrow and Glen canyons to Lee's Ferry, including the San Juan River below Chinle Creek. Issued in 1922, the maps showed the rivers, including the rapids, on a large scale (2" = one mile) and adjacent topography up to the 3,900-foot level. These were the first accurate maps of the rivers and the canyons, and they were highly useful to the growing numbers of boaters floating the rivers. The maps also helped stabilize the canyon nomenclature.

The work of the mapmakers was preliminary to that of the dam builders. When the Colorado near Yuma broke its banks in 1905, governments and private interests began to search for ways to control and harness the river, and for ways to divide its waters among the seven states of the Colorado River Basin. The long "War for the Colorado" was settled in 1922 when representatives of the seven states signed the Colorado River Compact. This agreement divided the water between the Upper Basin states (Utah, Wyoming, Colorado, New Mexico) and the Lower Basin states (Arizona, California, Nevada), the point of division being fixed at Lee's Ferry. The compact resolved the complex issues of rights to the water in a land where water is scarce. It established the basis for future agreements between the compact states, and it opened the way for federally-funded multipurpose reclamation projects. The Lower Basin moved rapidly. The Boulder Canyon Project Act of 1928 gave us Hoover Dam, completed in 1935.

In 1948, the Upper Basin states finally agreed on a formula for the division of their share of the water available to them under the compact. Now they faced this problem: The volume of water flowing down the Colorado fluctuates from year to year, but the compact specified that the Lower Basin should annually receive its share of the long-time average flow even in years when the runoff was below normal. Solution? Conventional thinking at the time called for a system of major reservoirs in the Upper Basin to provide for long-term holdover storage. Thus, downstream requirements could be met and the compact allotment to the Upper Basin would be guaranteed.

In 1952, the Bureau of Reclamation completed a masterplan for the development of water resources of the Upper Basin, and it was this plan which, after extended debate, testimony, comment, and hearings, was signed into law April 11, 1956, thus creating the Colorado River Storage Project. The law authorized four major dams. A fifth, proposed for Echo Park on the Green River in Dinosaur National Monument, was deleted after spirited, national opposition by conservation groups and others, primarily because the dam would be an "invasion" of the national park system. There seems to have been little objection to the inclusion of Glen Canyon, the keystone unit of the entire project.

By 1956 the scenic, scientific, and recreational resources of Glen and San Juan canyons and of the adjacent territory, were generally well known; so well known that a proposal to create a national park, a monument, or recreation area embracing all of the territory had been studied, debated, and defeated during the years 1935-1940. This was the Escalante National Monument, not defeated through lack of suitable resources, but through the inability of federal and state agencies to find a way to consensus.

Further public awareness of the Glen Canyon region came when the U.S. National Park Service published a heavy quarto volume entitled *A Survey of the Recreational Resources of the Colorado River Basin*, compiled in 1946 and issued by the Government Printing Office in 1950. The contents of this rather remarkable document, complete with folding maps, covered the entire basin. One long chapter with many striking black-and-white photographs describes the "Canyon Lands of Southeastern Utah" and their recreational possibilities.

The quest for a national monument and the study of recreational resources helped to boost boating in Glen and San Juan canyons, already a popular sport by the 1940s. A pioneer in commercial river running was Norman D. Nevills. After one season with the elaborate Rainbow Bridge-Monument Valley Expedition, which sent no fewer than 11 boating parties down the San Juan and Colorado rivers (1933-1938), Nevills went on to develop a successful river tour business based at Mexican Hat. With flair and a style appealing to the "dudes," Nevills ran popular trips and he enjoyed some good publicity from the pens of his passengers. After World War II, commercial tours increased as Harry Aleson, Don Harris, Georgie White, Art Greene, and others, started up operations. Commercial outfitters found they must share the quiet water of Glen Canyon with private parties, most of whom came riding their own war-surplus, inflatable, neoprene rubber rafts powered by outboard motors, usually of low horsepower.

I joined their growing numbers in 1949 when Salt Lake realtor O. Coleman Dunn invited me to make a run from Hite to Lee's Ferry. With the Geological Survey's 1922 river maps in hand, I went to see Bert Loper at his home in Green River. Bert was finishing up work on a boat he was building to take him through Grand Canyon that summer on his 80th birthday. Bert had been on the river for many years; he knew it as well as any man. In recent years he had served as guide for Boy Scout groups boating through Glen Canyon. He gave me much important information and some practical advice on navigation.

On a second trip through the canyon in 1950 I was accompanied by Professor David E. Miller, colleague in history at the University of Utah. On both trips we used ten-man rubber rafts which worked wonderfully well in the canyons. They'd bounce off rocks, crawl over rapids, and you could beach them in water inches deep. Sometimes the purists in hard-bottom craft would call them "baloney" boats, but the homely neoprene rafts with their sausage-like appearance, carried most of the river tourists through Glen and San Juan canyons during the post-war years.

During the passage through Glen Canyon we were enveloped in beauty all the way: the meandering river, its banks lined with plant life, the majestic red cliffs and terraces, the narrow side canyons, the amphitheaters, alcoves, glades, and glens, that suggested to Powell the name Glen Canyon. We found the canyon haunted, full of history. Bert Loper had said that it was, and we found out for ourselves. On the two trips we stopped at places echoing a page or two of history: Loper's cabin at the Hermitage, Cass Hite's ranch at Ticaboo, ruins of the great flume at Good Hope, mining equipment at California Bar, register names on the cliff at Hall's Crossing, the pioneer road at Hole-in-the-Rock, the names of the Powell expedition at Music Temple, the long picked-out trail to Klondike Bar, the Spanish steps at the Crossing of the Fathers, and the panel of prehistoric petroglyphs at Wright Bar. There were other places too, with intriguing names—Dandy Crossing, Moqui Canyon, Wasp House, Hidden Passage, Dangling Rope Canyon, Wild Horse Bar.

What men had passed through this wilderness of rivers and canyons and left these names on the land? For me the perfect travel experience requires a beautiful land and a land full of ghosts. Was there a history here to match the lavish beauty of the canyon? Yes, there was. I found the human story in bits and pieces. No one had put them all together before 1956 when the Colorado River Storage Project Act became law. This called for the construction of Glen Canyon Dam, the key unit of the project. When the National Park Service began to formulate plans for salvage studies in the reservoir area, I urged that adequate study be made of the historical resources jeopardized by the construction. I was indeed happy to accept responsibility for the work in historical archeology. This was part of a comprehensive salvage program, which included archeology and ecology as well as history, sponsored by the National Park Service and carried out by the University of Utah, Salt Lake City, and the Museum of Northern Arizona, Flagstaff.

My objective was to locate and record historical sites that would be lost to the waters of Lake Powell. Given the extent of the reservoir area, this was a sizeable undertaking. With important contributions by good friends, colleagues, and university students the field studies begun in 1957 were completed in 1963 when the gates were closed at Glen Canyon Dam. Nearly all of the fieldwork was done by boat. We went through San Juan, Cataract, and Narrow canyons a number of times and through Glen Canyon, the richest in history, a dozen times or so. We recorded well over 200 historical sites. At the same time, project archeologists recorded some 2,000 prehistoric sites.

How do you locate historical sites? Well, drifting along in a boat you could see the obvious ones from the river. Documentary sources and living informants led you to others. Another method was to look for them while walking over slickrock, sandbars, and gravel terraces. There was some work involved, if you can call it that, but there was always the river—the camp on the white sand beach in the shade of a towering cliff, the beauty of the water, and the rays of the setting sun rising on the opposite cliff.

This book, a capsule history of Glen and San Juan canyons, describes and portrays some of the most interesting places we saw during those years in the canyons. In addition to the possibilities for home reading, if you like to mix history and natural beauty as I do, these pages may enhance your pleasure while boating on the lake.

The author and the late David E. Miller (right) at the Crossing of the Fathers in the spring of 1959.

A.E. TURNER/BUREAU OF RECLAMATION

17

Two miles below the mouth of Dangling Rope Canyon the cliffs of Glen Canyon soared 1600 feet above the Colorado River.

C. GREGORY CRAMPTON

SECTION II

WAHWEAP TO RAINBOW BRIDGE

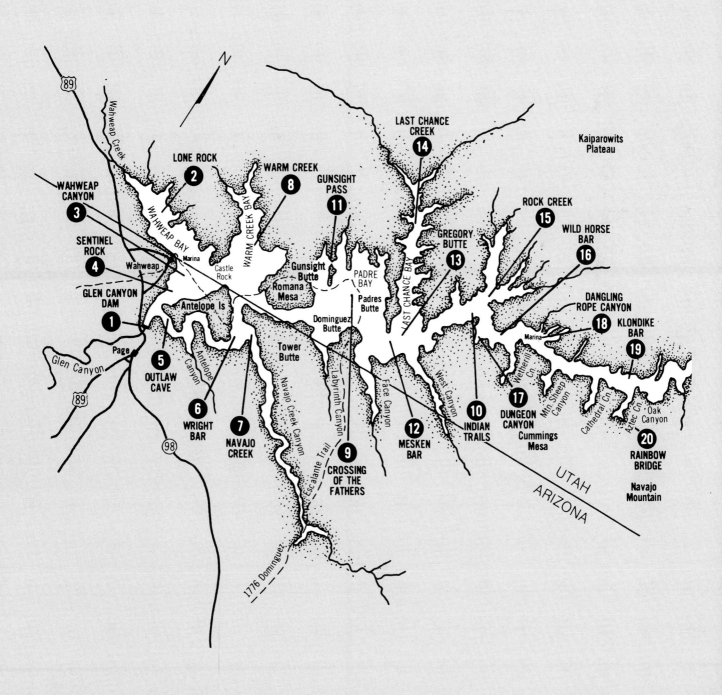

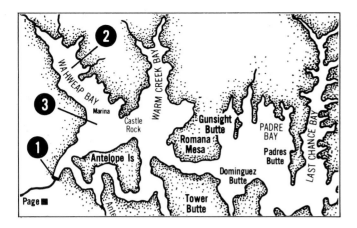

1 Glen Canyon Dam

Glen Canyon Dam in a nutshell: The dam is the key unit of the massive Colorado River Storage Project created by Congress to insure equitable distribution of the river's waters to each of the seven states of the Colorado River Basin. Some basic facts: authorized April 11, 1956; built by U.S. Bureau of Reclamation; first bucket of concrete, June 17, 1960; gates closed and Lake Powell begins to form March 13, 1963; last bucket of concrete, September 13, 1963; dedication, September 22, 1966; Carl Hayden Visitor Center, overlooking the dam, dedicated, 1968.

2 Lone Rock

Now a monolithic island near the head of Wahweap Bay, Lone Rock was a favorite camping place for stockmen ranging cattle down the Wahweap drainage where in the 1880s and 1890s the grass was stirrup high. Cattle were put out on the open country now covered by the wide waters between Wahweap Bay and Padre Bay. The big rock stood on the bank of Wahweap Creek and towered some 474 feet above it. Some of the cowboys with time to kill decorated the base of the rock with their names, brands, and other graffiti. The lake's high-water mark inundates 140 feet of Lone Rock leaving 334 feet exposed.

3 Wahweap Canyon

A long, intermittent stream, heading on the Kaiparowits Plateau, Wahweap (a Paiute Indian word meaning alkaline seeps or pools) Creek flowed through a fairly open valley, save for the last three or four miles where, fed by copious springs, it ran through a deeply entrenched canyon before reaching the Colorado. The lower passage between the Wahweap Marina and the main body of Lake Powell covers the canyon of the Wahweap. For decades Glen Canyon river runners stopped at the mouth of the canyon to refresh themselves with the delightful cool spring waters of the Wahweap.

Visitors look over Glen Canyon damsite in June of 1956, shortly after authorization of the Colorado River Storage Project.

Looking upstream toward completed Glen Canyon Dam and highway bridge on U.S. 89.

C. GREGORY CRAMPTON

A.E. TURNER/BUREAU OF RECLAMATION

C. GREGORY CRAMPTON

Top, Lone Rock on Wahweap Creek was a camping spot popular with local cattlemen. Above, an example of cowboy graffiti on the base of Lone Rock. Left, spring water flows from the base of 75-foot-high walls in the narrow canyon of the Wahweap.

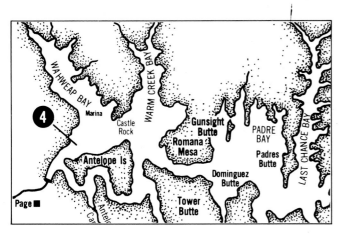

4 Sentinel Rock

Before the dam, Wahweap Creek flowed into the Colorado at the base of a huge slab of rock rising some 200 feet above the riverbank. The top of the rock is now about 355 feet below the surface of Lake Powell. For over 80 years the huge rock, standing out boldly from the adjoining cliff of which it was once a part, was one of the landmarks in Glen Canyon best known to river runners.

The rock was named and first described by members of the second Powell expedition who camped at its base in October, 1871. E.O. Beaman took some photographs. One of the photos was made into an engraving by renowned artist Thomas Moran and published by Powell in his *Report* of the second expedition published in 1875. Moran's fanciful engraving, captioned "Island Monument in Glen Canyon," portrayed the rock as an isolated pillar standing near the middle of the river.

A few river travelers, familiar with Powell's 1875 book, complained that the "Island" was nowhere to be found. Frederick S. Dellenbaugh, youngest member of Powell's party set the record straight when he published Beaman's original photo of the rock in his *Canyon Voyage* first issued in 1908.

Most river people, among them Bert Loper, were little concerned with such trivia. Loper, prospector and well-known river man, who came to know the Colorado River as well as anyone, thought of Sentinel Rock as an appropriate place for his signature. And so, on the creek side of the rock, he recorded his passages through Glen Canyon over a span of 41 years (1907-1948). In 1949, in his 80th year, Loper lost his life on a run through Grand Canyon.

The other names—Russell G. Frazier, Charles Kelly and Byron Davies—located the Spanish steps at the Crossing of the Fathers, and in 1938 they placed a plaque marking the crossing. (See No. 9)

A.E. TURNER/BUREAU OF RECLAMATION

J.W. POWELL, EXPLORATION (1875)

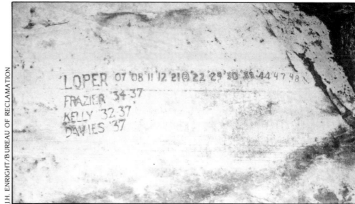

J.H. ENRIGHT/BUREAU OF RECLAMATION

Top, Thomas Moran's "Island Monument" as it appeared in Powell's **Report** *of his second expedition. Above, Bert Loper's register at the base of Sentinel Rock.*

Boaters photograph towering Sentinel Rock, the top of which is now about 355 feet below the surface of Lake Powell.

23

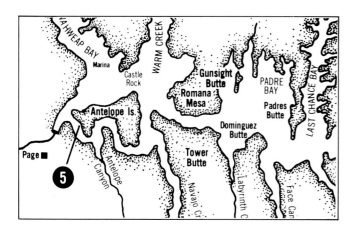

5 Galloway Cave

During the river days, Galloway Cave, less than half a mile above Sentinel Rock, was a natural and popular camping place for boating parties. This was a "royal arch" cave about 80 feet long and 25 feet deep. It was close to the riverbank; the floor of the cave was about ten feet above the high-water mark. The flat back wall was an invitation to campers to inscribe their names. One of the earlier autographs was that of "N. Galloway," done in charcoal, and the date "January 6, 1894."

Now Nathaniel T. Galloway was a well-known prospector, trapper, and boatman. In his canyon travel he developed the stern first technique in fast-water navigation and the light "Galloway-type" boat which was used with success by Julius F. Stone who hired Galloway as head boatman for a run through the canyons from Green River, Wyoming, to Needles, California, in 1909. Stone made the trip primarily in the spirit of adventure and travel, one of the first tourist runs through the canyons. Apparently, the Stone party did not stop at the cave, but Galloway spun out a yarn about it for the benefit of the passengers. Some time ago, Galloway said, he was running down the river when a severe storm came up. He ducked into the cave for shelter. But the river rose as the storm continued, and the water trapped him within the shelter, rising until it touched his chin. At that point, the water subsided and allowed Galloway to escape. Galloway was a good storyteller and a good boatman, a combination traditional among commercial river men since his time.

Nathaniel Galloway was a connecting link between the mining and tourist years in Glen Canyon history. Prompted by his experience on the river, later boatmen, using Galloway's fast-water methods and boats, began to develop recreational traffic on a wide scale. One such was Norman Nevills, who began running the San Juan and Colorado rivers in the 1930s. Nevills made Galloway Cave one of the camping places for his expeditions and named it Outlaw Cave. There was a rumor that a horse thief had hidden out in the place for a time. A name like that would stir up the imaginations of the passengers, Nevills knew, and enliven the campfire entertainment. Nevills' name for the cave stuck although some other river men thought that Galloway Cave was more appropriate.

A.E. TURNER/BUREAU OF RECLAMATION

A.E. TURNER/BUREAU OF RECLAMATION

Nathaniel Galloway's signature in Galloway Cave.

Historical research party photographs Galloway Cave, popular camping place in Lower Glen Canyon.

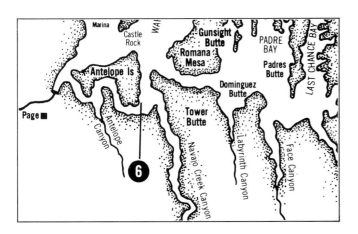

6 Wright Bar

Wright Bar was distinguished in Glen Canyon history as the site of a magnificent 50-foot panel of ancient petroglyphs pecked into the smooth face of a cliff overlooking the Colorado River. The panel contained dozens of figures and designs making up a style which may date anywhere from about 100 B.C. to about 1050 A.D., the oldest style of rock art in Glen Canyon.

Rock art, a term used to describe pecked or incised figures and designs (petroglyphs) and painted figures and designs (pictographs), is found widely in the Southwest and elsewhere. On cliffs and walls and huge blocks of rock at the foot of talus slopes, Indian artists found countless attractive surfaces on which to practice their craft. Many rock art sites in Glen Canyon, numbering perhaps in the hundreds, have been covered by Lake Powell. We will portray some of them in this book. Although most of these rock drawings were made by pre-Columbian or prehistoric peoples, modern Indians, notably Navajos, and white men have added their own drawings and inscriptions. As for pre-Columbian rock art: What do the figures, designs, and drawings mean? How does one read them? These are difficult questions since the artist's intent or purpose is quite elusive and we have no written record explaining the artist's views. But in many sites, some design elements, notably animals, are readily identifiable.

Wright Bar was also a mining site. During the Glen Canyon gold rush this was one of the few places where placer gold was found in the low water sandbars rather than in gravel terraces. A shallow cave here was a favored camping spot for numbers of miners and boaters. The signatures of several Glen Canyon characters were found on the sides of the cave. Among them: G.M. Wright; E. Mesken, 1892; A.G. Turner, 1896-1912; Bert Loper, 1908; Kolb Brothers, 1911, 1921, 1923, 1928.

In 1911-1912, Ellsworth and Emery Kolb, photographers at Grand Canyon, boated from Green River, Wyoming, to Needles, California, making movies of the rivers and the canyons. The Kolbs found Glen Canyon nearly deserted, but they saw much evidence of the recent mining boom. Ellsworth Kolb's straightforward narrative of the brothers' trip was published in book form in 1914 and reprinted frequently. As the inscription indicates, the Kolbs revisited Glen Canyon several times. In 1921, they were employed as boatmen by the U.S. Geological Survey party mapping Cataract, Narrow, Glen, and San Juan canyons. The river maps produced by the survey were used by boatmen and engineers for decades. For those sections of the rivers not flooded by Lake Powell, the maps are still in use.

A.E. TURNER/BUREAU OF RECLAMATION

Prehistoric artists, using stone on stone, pecked out this elaborate panel of petroglyphs at Wright Bar.

A.E. TURNER-BUREAU OF RECLAMATION

This inscription by the Kolb Brothers at Wright Bar recorded four trips in Glen Canyon.

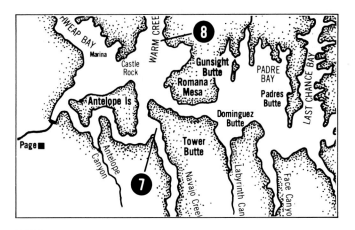

7 Navajo Creek

Navajo Creek, a long eastern tributary of the Colorado, entered the river ten miles above the Glen Canyon damsite. Throughout its lower reach the creek flowed through a narrow canyon, now a serpentine arm of Lake Powell about 18 miles long. For its entire length, the canyon was passable by foot, and it was an aboriginal route between the plateau country to the east and the Colorado River. Members of the second Powell expedition camped at the creek's mouth on October 17, 1871, where they found pieces of pottery and arrowheads left by prehistoric people.

8 Warm Creek

Under the waters of Lake Powell, at the mouth of Warm Creek Bay, lies a group of rock buildings, a monument to the entrepreneurial spirit of one Charles H. Spencer. In 1910 eight rock structures were built here as part of an extensive mining enterprise centered at Lee's Ferry (See No. 66). Undertaken by a Chicago corporation and managed by Spencer, the company planned to work the gravels and the colorful Chinle Formation, both of which contained small amounts of gold. Previously, on the San Juan River, Spencer had attempted with little success to extract gold from the crushed rock of the orange-red Wingate Sandstone. When it was discovered that the Chinle Formation also contained gold, Spencer moved the operation to Lee's Ferry where there was a large outcrop of this formation.

To operate the machinery at the new location, Spencer located and developed two coal mines on an upper fork of Warm Creek and then put up this cluster of buildings to serve as a transportation base and coal depot. Coal brought down from the mines was loaded on wagons at this point and hauled down through the narrow canyon of Warm Creek to the Colorado River.

In order to move the coal to Lee's Ferry, 28 miles distant, Spencer's company assembled a large steamboat, named the "Charles H. Spencer," at the mouth of Warm Creek from parts brought in from San Francisco. It required $30,000 and six months to get the parts to the site and to prepare the boat for launching, which took place in February, 1912. Excepting the huge gold dredge upstream, built ten years earlier by the Hoskaninni Company, the "Spencer" was the largest craft ever operated in Glen Canyon. It was 92 feet long, with a 25-foot beam, and was driven by a 12-foot stern paddle wheel powered by a steam boiler ten feet long. The boat was a failure. After five trips she was tied up at Lee's Ferry and not used again. The company operated for a few months in 1911 and 1912. Not enough gold was saved to pay costs. Operations were suspended, and the buildings on Warm Creek were abandoned.

Charles H. Spencer's coal depot on Warm Creek, 1910.

RUSHO COLLECTION

A.E. TURNER/BUREAU OF RECLAMATION

A.E. TURNER/BUREAU OF RECLAMATION

A.E. TURNER/BUREAU OF RECLAMATION

Top, modern explorer views the mouth of Navajo Creek, a major Colorado River tributary in Glen Canyon. Above, government surveyors rest on the remains of a crude structure probably built by prospectors working at Wright Bar, across the river from the mouth of Navajo Creek.

A.E. TURNER/BUREAU OF RECLAMATION

The ruins of Spencer's coal depot on Warm Creek, now covered by about 250 feet of water.

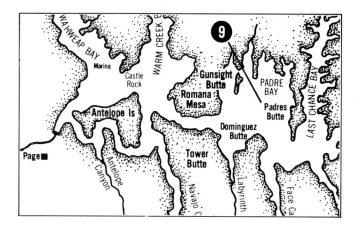

9 The Crossing of the Fathers

The recorded history of Glen Canyon began in 1776 when a small, Spanish exploring party headed by two Franciscan friars, Francisco Atanasio Dominguez and Silvestre Velezde Escalante, reached the Colorado at Lee's Ferry. Starting from Santa Fe they had hoped to open a road between New Mexico and California and to locate sites for missions and settlements en route. The explorers passed through western Colorado and central Utah. They had started late, and when they reached south-central Utah, bad weather forced them to turn back to New Mexico. Heading eastward the padres worked their way across the Arizona Strip and finally reached the confluence of the Paria and Colorado Rivers where nearly a hundred years later John D. Lee opened the ferry named after him.

The Spaniards were in a tight fix. They had to find a way across the river, but the Colorado ran swift, deep, and cold. Their attempts to ford and to paddle across on crude crafts failed. Desperate now, they started out to look for a place to cross the river higher up. The first week in November, 1776, was the worst of their entire trip. They were low on food; the weather was foul. From the Lee's Ferry campsite, the explorers, with great difficulty, managed to work their way up the Echo Cliffs. Cresting the ridge through Dominguez Pass, they headed downhill over the long slope where deep red sand and rocky arroyos slowed their passage. Reaching a stream of potable water, and with pasturage at hand, the padres went into camp, naming it "San Diego." Their campsite, now covered by Lake Powell, was on Wahweap Creek, a few yards from the present Wahweap Resort. The expedition diarist noted that a jumble of rocks resembling the "ruins of a fortress" were visible from their camp—the first description of Castle Rock and other unnamed formations standing above the water directly across the bay from the lodge.

Now they went on to reach the rim of Glen Canyon opposite the mouth of Navajo Creek, but they could not get down to the river some 500 feet below (See No. 7). Scouting ahead, one of the men returned to say he had found a passage to the river through a narrow side canyon. Pressing on, the Spaniards stopped at the base of the high, prominent Romana Mesa, which name derives from the name they gave their campsite, Santa Francisca Romana. Next, camp was in the shadow of the towering Gunsight Butte. From there, the scout led the party down through the canyon (now called Padre) to a sandbar on the river's edge. To keep the animals from slipping at one point in the descent, step-like grooves, or footholds, were chipped into the steepest slope.

The river was found to be shallow enough to wade but the friars rode across on horseback. By five o'clock in the afternoon of November 7, the entire party of 13 men had forded the Colorado. They celebrated, wrote Escalante in his diary, "by praising God, our Lord, and firing off a few muskets as a sign of the great joy we all felt at having overcome so great a difficulty." The ford was named on the spot: La

Looking downstream toward the actual ford at the Crossing of the Fathers. From the mouth of Padre Creek (not visible) near the head of the sandbar, travelers crossed diagonally coming out on a low sandbank just beyond the rocky slope on the left. The ford could be used only when the river was low and the sandbar exposed. In the distance stand Line Rock or Boundary Butte (left), and Tower Butte.

To reach a ford on the Colorado, Spanish explorers chopped steps on a steep slope of Padre Canyon to prevent the animals from falling. Steps appear to the left of two lower figures.

C. GREGORY CRAMPTON

Descending the steep slopes of Padre Canyon, the 1937 Frazier-Kelly-Davies party re-locates the Crossing of the Fathers.

UTAH STATE HISTORICAL SOCIETY

Purisima Concepcion de la Virgen Santisima (the Immaculate Conception of the Most Holy Virgin). This was the first recorded Colorado crossing anywhere in the long line of great canyons below Moab, Utah, and the mouth of Grand Canyon, a distance of over 550 miles.

Once across the Colorado barrier, the Dominguez-Escalante expedition, following an Indian trail, headed south and east staying to the right of a long line of beautifully sculptured monuments. Within three days the Spaniards had reached and crossed the middle canyon of Navajo Creek, a very considerable barrier itself, at the extreme head of an arm of Lake Powell. The trail down to Navajo Creek was steep, but at the worst place, Escalante wrote in his diary, the Indians sometime before had built a "stairway" to permit passage to the creekbed. Beyond the canyon, and now in open country, the Spaniards headed for the Hopi villages and Santa Fe.

In their traverse of Glen Canyon the Spaniards had found a major Indian route which had been in use for at least 700 years. Even before the Normans invaded England in 1066, the prehistoric Anasazi Indians were crossing back and forth across the Colorado River here.

After 1776, the ford was used intermittently for nearly a century. Mexican traders, Mormon missionaries, government explorers (see back cover), and Navajo Indians came this way. On early maps the crossing bore the Spanish name "El Vado de los Padres" (Ford of the Fathers), but in modern times Spanish has given way to the English, "Crossing of the Fathers."

With the opening of Lee's Ferry after 1872, the ford fell into disuse, and its exact location was "lost" for years. Finally, as a result of some on-the-ground field work, the crossing was relocated and publicized by Dr. Russell G. Frazier, Charles Kelly, and Byron Davies, and in 1938 a plaque was placed by them on the canyon wall at the mouth of Padre Creek. The plaque was removed before it was covered by the rising waters of Lake Powell.

The exploration by Dominguez and Escalante was a remarkable achievement. Not only were they discoverers of Glen Canyon, but the records they made are the earliest we have descriptive of much of the upper basin of the Colorado River. The diary kept by the padres, full as it is of geographical, ethnological, and biological information, and the beautiful charts made by Bernardo de Miera y Pacheco, expedition cartographer, literally put the region they explored on the map. The full diary account of the expedition has been published in two readily available editions: Bolton, ed. (1950), and Chavez, trans., Warner, ed. (1976). See also Briggs (1976).

The line in this aerial photograph traces the route of the 1776 Spanish expedition after crossing the Colorado River. Padres Butte (center, left) is now an island in Lake Powell.

Pottery found by the author in a shallow cave on an old Indian trail used by Dominguez and Escalante in 1776. The artifacts are now in the Museum of Northern Arizona, Flagstaff.

C. GREGORY CRAMPTON

Indian trail leading to Crossing of the Fathers. An abandoned Navajo hogan appears (upper center, left). Padres Butte dominates the skyline.

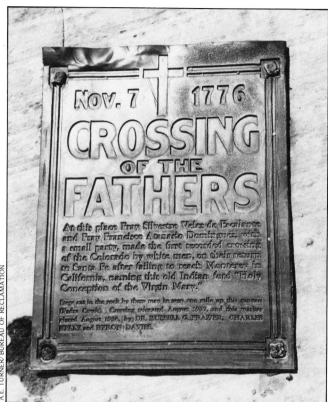

A.E. TURNER/ BUREAU OF RECLAMATION

Plaque placed in 1938 to mark the Crossing of the Fathers.

C. GREGORY CRAMPTON

Riding down this old Indian "stairway" in 1776, Dominguez and Escalante reached the bed of Navajo Creek, now under the water of Lake Powell.

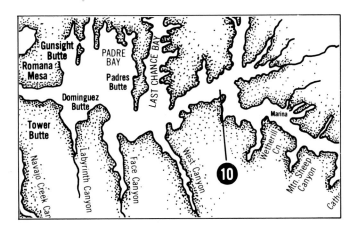

10 Indian Trails

The intricate, eroded landscape of the Glen Canyon region was no real barrier to prehistoric man. The canyon environment offered resources not found elsewhere, if at all. In a desert land, water was of first importance. There were useful plants and animals, and patches of arable land which could be irrigated. One additional resource of unusual significance was the river terrace gravels brought down the Colorado by melt water from Ice-age glaciers in the Rocky Mountains. In a region of soft sedimentary rocks, material suitable for making arrow points, knives, scrapers, and tools was scarce. To reach these resources, the Anasazis worked out trail systems running from the uplands down to the canyon bottoms. In some places cross-canyon trails were developed. Prehistoric trails were found in many places in Glen and San Juan Canyons, but they were most frequently seen in the lower reaches of Glen Canyon, notably, in the area now covered by Lake Powell's wide waters between Wahweap Bay and Rock Creek Bay.

What did an Anasazi trail look like? Not having iron tools, the Indians laboriously pecked out foothold steps often over breathtakingly steep surfaces. The smooth cup-like steps were not more than four inches wide and two inches deep, the minimum required to keep one from falling.

Centuries after the Anasazis had gone, the Navajo and Paiute Indians moved into the canyon country and used some of the old trails to reach the river bottoms. With picks and sharp-pointed tools, they enlarged the old steps or picked out new ones alongside them. Since the riverbars were good places to graze and water sheep, goats, and horses, the Indians in many places built ingenious stock trails to cross the steepest slopes.

Prehistoric man pecked steps in the Crossing of the Fathers area. The trail maker pecked out no more steps than absolutely necessary.

Three sets of trails are shown along this centuries-old staircase opposite the mouth of Rock Creek. The oldest, on the left, consists of small cups pecked out by prehistoric people. In the center are old steps picked out and enlarged by modern Indians. The Navajo stock trail was built in 1958-1959.

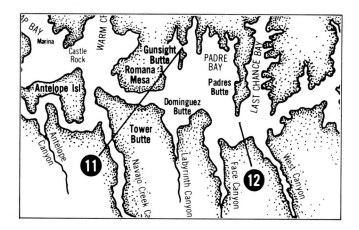

11 Gunsight Pass

Here lies a narrow, V-shaped passage resembling a rear rifle sight, bisecting the narrow peninsula-like mesa of which Gunsight Butte is the extremity. About 180 feet long, and wide enough to accommodate one man or one horse at a time, it was long the most frequently traveled approach to Padre Canyon and the Crossing of the Fathers, although Dominguez and Escalante missed it in 1776. In recent times, stockmen trailed cattle through the pass to reach rangeland now covered by Padre Bay. Some of the cowboys lingered to carve their names and brands on the steep walls. The floor of the pass is about 3,680 feet, some 20 feet below the maximum level of Lake Powell.

12 Mesken Bar

This was home to one of lower Glen Canyon's earliest residents, Denver prospector and trapper, Edward "Colorado Ed" Mesken, who staked a claim here in 1889. When he wasn't panning for gold he would leisurely travel up and down the river in a small boat with a small dog. Here and there he left his signature on the canyon walls.

A.E. TURNER/BUREAU OF RECLAMATION

A man standing at the point of the "V" is dwarfed by the massive western gateway to Gunsight Pass.

Left, hikers walk up over the slickrock trail toward the eastern entrance to Gunsight Pass. Above, from their camp on the riverbank, these river travelers could see in the distance the wooded outline of Mesken Bar.

C. GREGORY CRAMPTON

37

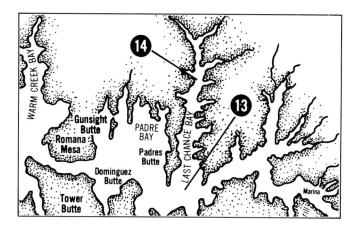

13 Gregory Butte

Gregory Butte, a majestic formation, now an island rising nearly a thousand feet above the surface of Lake Powell, was named for geologist Herbert E. Gregory (1869-1952). Among his many scientific publications, Gregory wrote five geological monographs blanketing the entire southern section of the Glen Canyon region; all were published as professional papers by the U.S. Geological Survey between 1915 and 1951. In these studies, based on extensive field work, he devoted much space to human history and geographical features often lacking in literature bearing the geological label. Gregory's monographs on the Navajo country, the Kaiparowits Plateau, and the San Juan region should be counted among the basic books on the canyon country.

14 Last Chance Creek

Last Chance Creek is a long tributary heading on the Kaiparowits Plateau. For several miles above its mouth the stream ran through an open valley that is now an extensive embayment of Lake Powell. For a few years, around the turn of the century, stockmen ran cattle through the valley, but this remote, dry, and fragile range probably gave out after a few seasons. Public land surveyors noted that a round-up camp on Last Chance was in ruins in 1934.

Top, west face of Gregory Butte before the dam. Middle, boating party stuck on a river sandbar under the shadow of Gregory Butte (east side). At this point, Lake Powell is now 500 feet deep. Above, U.S. Geological Survey and Reclamation Service officials stop for lunch in September of 1922, along the river opposite Gregory Butte, then called Church Rock. They were investigating possible dam sites.

Abandoned cattle camp on Last Chance Creek.

The place where Last Chance Creek entered the Colorado through a shallow canyon.

39

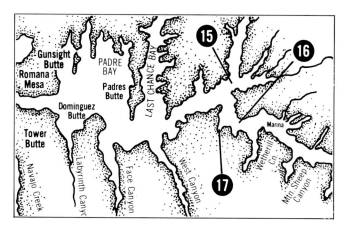

15 Rock Creek

Rock Creek, with its three forks, bites deeply into the Kaiparowits Plateau. The three-pronged bay now covering the lower parts of the forks is one of superlative beauty.

16 Wild Horse Bar

Wild Horse Bar was so named in 1921 by a government mapping party when a wild dappled gray horse was seen at the river's edge. This was the uppermost point on the right bank of Glen Canyon accessible by land from the Crossing of the Fathers area. Following a trail along the river's rim, two prospectors, engaged to supply the second Powell expedition, reached the bar in September or October, 1871. As late as the 1950s, there was some evidence of cattle having been on the bar.

17 Dungeon Canyon

For many of those who knew the river, the favorite part of Glen Canyon was the section between Rock Creek and the mouth of the San Juan River. For 22 miles it reminded one of a grand avenue. Cliffs and walls, cascading slickrock slopes, and points and promontories rose on both sides. Most of the tributary streams reached the river through narrow, slot-like canyons.

Top, smooth, rounded domes at the mouth of Rock Creek, now under 500 feet of water. Above, a Glen Canyon river traveler stops to explore the magic beauty of Dungeon Canyon.

C. GREGORY CRAMPTON

Looking downstream toward Wild Horse Bar.

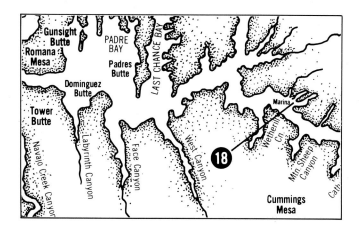

18 Dangling Rope Canyon

Now the site of the newest marina on Lake Powell, Dangling Rope Canyon heads on the southern extremity of the lofty Kaiparowits Plateau. Dangling Rope? Yes, there was one. Some river runners promptly named the canyon when they found a rope dangling down over a 40-foot slope. At the same place there were 19 or 20 picked steps, possibly of prehistoric origin though they had been enlarged by later users. When I visited the site a cottonwood log was standing below the steps making it possible for an agile person to reach the lowest one. Our party did not attempt to climb the trail, given the shallow toe-hold steps and the uncertain condition of the rope. We concluded that the route had been used by a prospecting party during the uranium boom after World War II.

Top, the dangling rope and steps in Dangling Rope Canyon. Above, the rope, probably left by a prospecting party during the uranium boom after World War II, hung over a 40-foot slope.

A hiker surveys the inner beauty of the west fork of Dangling Rope Canyon.

C. GREGORY CRAMPTON

43

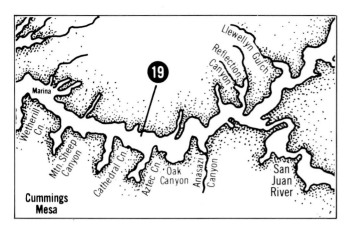

19 Klondike Bar

An extensive gravel bar on the right bank of the river, Klondike Bar was an important gold mining site in lower Glen Canyon. The location was staked in December, 1897, by Louis M. Chaffin, William B. "Billy" Hay, and others who named their claim for the contemporary gold rush to the Klondike in the Yukon. When I visited the site there was evidence of extensive mining activity which must have lasted several years: abandoned scrapers, ore trucks, flumes, sluice boxes, tools. The floor of a shallow cave was littered with chips left by prehistoric Indians who used the plentiful gravel on the bar to fashion arrow points and stone tools.

At the upper end of the bar a pole gate controlled access to a spectacular stock trail. From the bar the trail wound about over slickrock to top out 800 feet above the river at the base of a prominent butte which I have called Klondike Point. This was probably the longest and most elaborate stock trail in Glen Canyon. Cantilever construction was used to cross the steepest parts immediately above the river. Over other spots, platform steps, some in long series, were picked out. Indeed, platform steps, on the steepest slopes were found on the Klondike Trail in eight different places. One long series may be seen by boaters on the shore of Lake Powell.

Supplies and equipment destined for Klondike Bar were brought in from Escalante, Utah, via the Hole-in-the-Rock Trail to Fifty Mile Point on the eastern side of the Kaiparowits Plateau. Then, by following approximately the contour between 4,000 feet and 4,500 feet, the trail eventually reached Klondike Point by skirting the extended fingers of the Kaiparowits and by heading the tributary canyons of the Colorado between them. The full length of the trail from Escalante was probably about 85 long miles. For the mining activity we have no production figures.

W.L. RUSHO

Sunrise on the Colorado at Klondike Bar.

C. GREGORY CRAMPTON

Hiker surveys Klondike Bar, gold mining site in Glen Canyon.

Hikers pick their way along a narrow notch of what remained in this section of the trail to Klondike Bar.

Far left, hikers climb a long series of platform steps high on Klondike Trail. Left, Lake Powell waters lap at the base of the same trail. Klondike Point is in background.

45

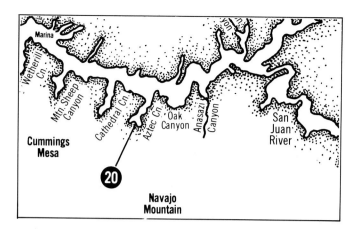

20 Rainbow Bridge

Rainbow Bridge, grandest of the world's natural bridges and located deep in the maze of canyons on the northwest flank of Navajo Mountain, was not known to the general public before 1909. Credit for the discovery belongs to Dean Byron Cummings of the University of Utah and to U.S. Surveyor W.B. Douglass. While conducting archeological investigations in northern Arizona, Cummings learned from the Wetherills, Indian traders at Kayenta, that the Indians knew of a natural bridge on the slopes of Navajo Mountain. With Nasja-begay, a Paiute Indian who knew the location, and John Wetherill as guides, Cummings set out to look for the stone bridge. En route he learned that W.B. Douglass, of the General Land Office was also looking for the bridge. With Douglass, as a guide, was Mike's Boy, a Paiute Indian. Cummings waited up for the Douglass party, and the two went on together passing around the rugged, dissected north side of Navajo Mountain. On August 14, 1909, they reached the magnificent arch.

On the spot, Douglass took the first set of measurements. With a span of 275 feet, the bridge gracefully arches to a height of 290 feet above the bed of Bridge Creek. At its highest point the arch is 42 feet thick and 33 feet wide. For many later visitors these measurements have held little meaning, for the bridge in its natural setting—within a canyon and at the foot of rugged Navajo Mountain—seems smaller than it really is.

On the day of discovery a few men walked down Bridge and Aztec Creeks to the Colorado River. There they found mining and camping equipment scattered about and what appeared to be some prehistoric structures at the mouth of the canyon. Prospectors working in Glen Canyon and exploring in the Navajo Mountain area were certainly the first whites to see the bridge, but they didn't bother to report the fact and, of course, the Indians had known of it for centuries. It was the Cummings-Douglass "discovery" in 1909 that led to the formation of Rainbow Bridge National Monument proclaimed by President Taft in 1910.

Visitors began to appear soon after the formation of the national monument. Guided by John Wetherill, both Theodore Roosevelt and Zane Grey arrived in 1913. For Roosevelt the bridge was "one of the wonders of the world." Grey said it was "glorious." Upon first view, he said, "It absolutely silenced me." Grey returned several times, for he found in the rugged canyon country inspiration for some of his best selling novels. Among others, *Riders of the Purple Sage, Heritage of the Desert,* and *Rainbow Trail* come to mind.

Charles L. Bernheimer, who described himself as "a tenderfoot and cliff-dweller from Manhattan," sponsored a number of exploratory and archeological expeditions into the Glen Canyon region between 1920 and 1930. In 1922 he reached the bridge and wrote that its symmetry, graceful sweep, balance, picturesque setting, and coloring make it a "unique and stupendous monument, a thing of beauty viewed from any angle" (from his book, *Rainbow Bridge,* published in 1924).

Another visitor in the 1920s was young Clyde Kluckhohn

MEL DAVIS/BUREAU OF RECLAMATION

Aerial view of the slickrock wilderness at the foot of Navajo Mountain. Can you locate Rainbow Bridge?

who went on to a distinguished career in anthropology. In his book, *To the Foot of the Rainbow,* he describes an adventurous, unguided horseback trip to Rainbow as the "uncomparable, the indescribable." When Kluckhohn arrived, a register book at the base of the bridge contained fewer than 200 names. Most of those visitors had packed in over the difficult trails around Navajo Mountain. Only a few had walked in from the river, a distance of 4.8 miles. Probably the first to do so were members of the U.S. Geological Survey mapping party who hiked up Aztec Creek, and the Bridge Creek, in 1921.

Aztec? This, along with Montezuma, is a fairly common name in the Southwest. Americans moving into the lands acquired from Mexico saw prehistoric ruins in many places. Some of the mid-19th century writers, among them William H. Prescott whose *History of the Conquest of Mexico* was widely read, had said that the Aztecs believed their place of beginning was somewhere in northern lands. Therefore, said the curious American, the ruins scattered around the Southwest must be structures left behind by those ancient Indians as they wandered southward. To prospectors working in Glen Canyon, the strange looking pillars at the mouth of the creek looked quite unlike anything they had seen elsewhere in the canyon so they gave the Aztecs credit for the structures and named the creek for the builders. The 1921 U.S. Geological mapping team accepted current usage and added another Aztec to the nomenclature of the Southwest! Originally there were four pillars at the site. Archeologists have found little evidence linking the structures to prehistoric people.

With the rapid growth of recreational travel on the Colorado after World War II, most visitors walked in from the river. But as late as 1949, their numbers were not large. On a ten-day boat trip through Glen Canyon in June of that year, our group hiked to Rainbow Bridge. We saw no other person. And we saw no other river party in all the distance between Hite and Lee's Ferry.

C. GREGORY CRAMPTON

Three men from a boating party in Glen Canyon hike up Aztec Creek to Rainbow Bridge.

Man stands under Rainbow Bridge, scenic lodestone of the Glen Canyon region.

C. GREGORY CRAMPTON

Structures of unknown origin at the mouth of Aztec Creek. Glen Canyon prospectors thought the Aztec Indians had built them.

The short canyon of Little Eden just below the mouth of Hall's Creek.

C. GREGORY CRAMPTON

RAINBOW BRIDGE TO BULLFROG AND HALL'S CROSSING

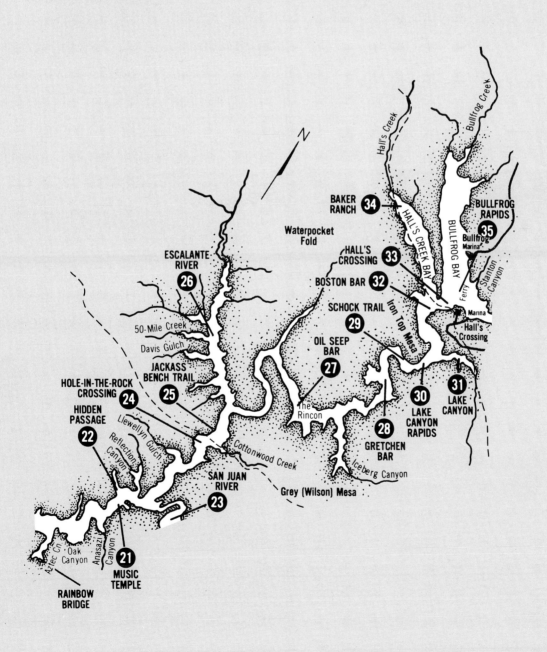

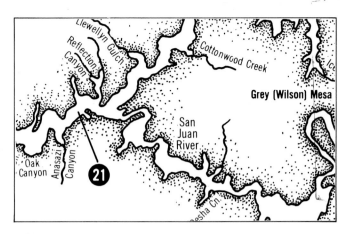

21 Music Temple

The first recorded exploration of Glen Canyon was accomplished by John Wesley Powell during the course of his two voyages on the Colorado in 1869 and 1871. Although Powell spent little time in Glen Canyon, crew members wrote about it at length, and most of their first-hand accounts have been published.

Near the mouth of a short, narrow canyon, Music Temple was a grotto-like chamber nearly arched over by high walls. There was a pool of water at the base of a normally dry waterfall. Ferns and mosses grew around the walls. The chamber was shaded and cool on the warmest day. Powell's 1869 expedition camped on the riverbank here August 1 and 2, and discovered and named it Music Temple. The sighing wind and the acoustical properties of the chamber suggested the name. After making some observations nearby, Powell took a long nap in the Temple while some of the men carved their names on a soft sandstone shelf.

The second Powell expedition nooned at Music Temple, October 5, 1871. While Powell climbed out to the rim of the canyon, some of the crew added their names to the sandstone register. Still others were added in 1872. Most of the names were still visible until covered by the rising waters of Lake Powell.

In a wilderness of naked rock, it was the cool, shady side canyons, caves and grottos, glens and alcoves, that John Wesley Powell chose to remember when he named it Glen Canyon, the place where so many of these features were found.

Names in Music Temple carved by members of the Powell expeditions, 1869-1872. C. Powell was Walter Clement "Clem" Powell, Major Powell's cousin; John K. "Jack" Hillers became a distinguished photographer for the Powell Survey and the U.S. Geological Survey; F.S. Dellenbaugh wrote important books on the Powell expeditions and Western history; and F.M. Bishop, topographer, made the first map of the Colorado River based upon actual measurement.

C. GREGORY CRAMPTON

C. GREGORY CRAMPTON

John Wesley Powell and his companions camped on this Glen Canyon beach, August 1 and 2, 1869. Nearby they found, described, and enjoyed idyllic Music Temple. On an August day 90 years later, another boating party stopped to visit Music Temple (behind the camera) and enjoy the beach.

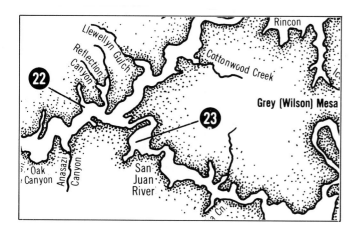

22 Hidden Passage

From the 1930s on, Hidden Passage was a popular stop and camping place for river runners. The narrow canyon mouth was all but hidden from the river, hence the name. The canyon was short but passage was possible up to about one mile from the mouth.

23 San Juan River

Heading in the Rocky Mountains of southwestern Colorado, the San Juan River is the longest tributary of the Colorado in Glen Canyon. Lake Powell, at 3,700 feet, covers the lower 70 miles of the river which form the longest arm of the lake. Something of the rich history of the flooded area will be found in Part V of this book.

C. GREGORY CRAMPTON

These hikers found they had to swim to reach the head of Hidden Passage.

Hidden Passage was like a ballet in sandstone.

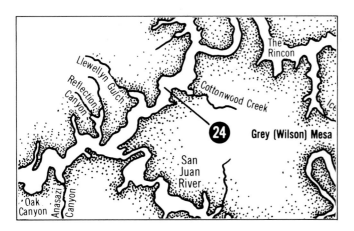

24 Hole-in-the-Rock Crossing

There is nothing quite like Hole-in-the-Rock in the history of the American West. Here, in early winter 1879-1880, an expedition organized under the auspices of the Mormon Church crossed Glen Canyon bound for southeastern Utah to colonize the sparsely settled areas along the San Juan River. This was the San Juan Mission which carried out a remarkable trek. Over 230 people—men, women, and children—in 83 wagons, driving over 1,000 head of livestock, traveled about 200 miles through country where wagons had never rolled before. Over most of this distance they had to build roads, miles of which were picked and blasted out of solid rock. Some of the more difficult places were Hole-in-the-Rock, Grey (Wilson) Mesa, Clay Hills, Grand Flat, and Comb Ridge. In April, 1880, the colonists reached a likely spot on the San Juan. From sheer exhaustion, they stopped and founded their settlement, calling it "Bluff." They had planned to be on the road six weeks. It took them six months. No lives were lost. Three babies were born along the way.

The most serious obstacle encountered on the trek was the descent over the west rim of Glen Canyon. At one point the pioneer band found a narrow crack, or slit, at the head of a short, steep canyon which opened out on the river less than a mile away. This must have seemed like something less than a feasible route, but they went ahead anyway. By blasting, the Mormons enlarged the crack wide enough for the passage of wagons and it has since been known as Hole-in-the-Rock.

Below the Hole the canyon widened somewhat, but there was no natural route. A road had to be built along the left side, some distance above the canyon bed. Narrow places were widened by blasting, picking away the sandstone rock and heavy talus, shoring up on the canyon side. At one place, where there was nothing more than a narrow ledge on a near perpendicular wall, oak stakes were set in the cliff, stringers were laid across these, and on top of them logs, brush, and rocks were used to make a road wide enough for wagons. A shelf for the inside wheels was picked from the side of the cliff.

The drop in elevation from the rim to the river was just over 1,000 feet. The average grade was about 25 percent but some sections approximated 45 percent! To prevent wagons from plunging ahead too fast on the descent, rear wheels were rough-locked, and holding onto ropes attached to the wagon, a dozen or so men pulled back as the wagon skidded and bumped down over the steepest places.

After crossing the river on a two-wagon ferry built by Charles Hall, the pioneers had to build a steep dugway on the opposite side to reach a wide bench some 300 feet above the Colorado. Once on the bench, where road building was also necessary, the expedition passed between Register Rocks, where some members inscribed their names. They shortly reached Cottonwood Creek, a meandering stream in an open valley. At this point, where there was good water, forage, and plenty of

Aerial view of the Hole-in-the-Rock Crossing of Glen Canyon. Wagons were driven (not lowered) through "hole" (a) down to the river and ferried across. A road was built up to the notch (b). Then it was comparatively easy going. The road passed between Register Rocks (c) to Cottonwood Creek (d).

A.E. TURNER/BUREAU OF RECLAMATION

W.L. RUSHO

In this 1963 photograph a boating party, riding the rising waters of Lake Powell, examined a section of the steep dugway opposite Hole-in-the-Rock. Teams pulled wagons up over the rocky road (above men at the boat) to a bench above the Colorado River.

C. GREGORY CRAMPTON

Looking up to the "hole" at Hole-in-the-Rock, where in 1879 the San Juan Mission pioneers blasted and picked out a crack in the canyon rim making it wide enough for the passage of wagons. Nineteen years later the Hoskaninni Mining Company cut the steps for use by men and pack animals.

wood, the pioneer band camped while another very difficult road was built to the top of Grey Mesa. The campsite was above the head of the pleasant inlet of Lake Powell covering the lower course of Cottonwood Creek.

The history of the Hole-in-the-Rock expedition, with full details about the route, is the subject of a scholarly and readable book by the late David E. Miller (1966).

For about a year after 1880 the rugged road across Glen Canyon was used as a main link between the new settlement at Bluff and the older communities west of the Colorado. Traffic over the road went both ways, although it is difficult to imagine that a wagon could be driven *up* through the Hole. Before the end of 1881 a new route had been found, reaching the Colorado at Hall's Crossing 35 miles upstream where Charles Hall operated a ferry service for about five years. (See No. 33.)

After the discovery of gold in Glen Canyon, the Hole-in-the-Rock crossing was a boon to prospectors since it offered them access to the river in a section of the canyon otherwise difficult to reach. Robert B. Stanton, head of the Hoskaninni Company, the largest mining company ever to operate along the Colorado, planned to use the Hole-in-the-Rock as a major gateway to the canyon. (See No. 36). To undertake assessment work, Stanton (in 1899), sent a party of 26 men under Nathaniel Galloway to improve the pioneer road and ready it for mining operations. By cutting steps from the Hole down over the slickrock sections, the roadbed was converted into a stairway suitable for pedestrians and pack animals. Some recent visitors to Hole-in-the-Rock have inaccurately thought the picked out steps were made by the Mormon pioneer groups.

The Hole-in-the-Rock crossing was much used by Indians— Navajos, Paiutes, Utes—to reach the white settlements west of the river and the hunting grounds on the Kaiparowits Plateau and elsewhere. To capitalize on the Indian trade, Henry N. Cowles and Joseph T. Hall opened a trading post in 1900, on the river at the foot of Hole-in-the-Rock canyon. For two years the partners carried on a lively trade, exchanging foodstuffs, tobacco, yardage, and hardware for hides, wool, and textiles. After Cowles and Hall left the river, their one-room trading post fell into ruins, later noted by many visitors. The structure was not built by the Mormon San Juan Mission, nor is it linked with Charles Hall who built and operated the ferry at this point in 1879-1880.

The historic Hole-in-the-Rock may be reached easily by boaters on Lake Powell, and it is accessible by road from the town of Escalante. Tourists visiting Hole-in-the-Rock today should realize that it has eroded considerably. Large rocks from the walls have fallen and choked the passage making it difficult to imagine that wagons were once driven down through the slot. The steps picked out by the Hoskaninni Company, 1899-1900, make the passage rather easy for pedestrians. At full pool, the lake is about 435 feet deep at the Hole-in-the-Rock Crossing, but most of the pioneer rock work on the road remains out of water.

Historical researcher studies construction details of Cowles and Hall trading post on the Colorado at the foot of Hole-in-the-Rock road.

C. GREGORY CRAMPTON

Once across the Colorado, and after more road construction (bottom), the San Juan Mission pioneers reached Register Rocks.

C. GREGORY CRAMPTON

Compare the scene above with this "after Lake Powell" photo taken in September of 1983. Now, in a boat, you can follow the pioneers through Register Rocks.

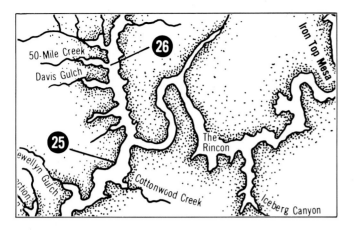

Sections of the Jackass Bench Trail are visible from Lake Powell. Note picked steps at water's edge (lower left). Man at upper right stands on a long series of steps picked in the sandstone.

25 Jackass Bench Trail

This well-built stock trail from the rim of Glen Canyon reaches the northern end of Jackass Bench, an elevated grazing area extending from Hole-in-the-Rock north along the river for some two miles. The Bench is now covered with water. The trail, consisting of picked steps and ledges over the steeper places, may be seen from the lake at a point about one mile north of the mouth of Hole-in-the-Rock inlet. Rock cairns mark the route on the upper sections. At the rim the trail doubles back to the head of Hole-in-the-Rock. The trail may have been built by the Hoskaninni Company in 1899-1900. It was used by miners, Indians, traders, and others to bypass the steep road through Hole-in-the-Rock.

26 Escalante River

A major tributary of the Colorado in Glen Canyon, the Escalante River drains a large basin bounded on the north by the lofty Boulder Mountain-Aquarius Plateau, on the west by the Kaiparowits Plateau, and on the east by the Waterpocket Fold. For approximately 70 miles of its lower course, this picturesque stream flows in a deep, twisting canyon. It receives water from springs and seeps and from numerous tributaries which, at their mouths, and usually for some distance, also flow through deep canyons. In a continuous series of graceful bends, the Escalante meanders around sandy terraces and beaches, past sandstone walls decorated with tapestries of desert varnish, past cottonwoods, willows, oaks, shady alcoves and verdant glens. The side canyons offer huge overhangs and amphitheaters, sandy streambeds lined with vegetation, delicate waterfalls spilling over smooth ledges, springs supporting lush carpets of flowers, ferns, and mosses.

A number of natural bridges and arches add to the beauty of the Escalante, thought by many to be one of the superlative canyon landscapes of the Colorado Plateau. Lake Powell has flooded about 27 miles of the lower Escalante, a straight-line distance of 12 miles.

In modern times history has touched the lower canyons of the Escalante but lightly. The name was applied to the river in 1872 by A.H. Thompson of the Powell Survey, who crossed the upper basin on an exploratory reconnaissance. Returning in 1875 to find some Mormons planning a settlement, Thompson suggested they call the place Escalante after the Spanish explorer. The Dominguez-Escalante expedition did not reach the Escalante drainage, but Thompson knew his history and wanted to see a first explorer of the rugged canyon country remembered.

Ever seeking additional range lands, the stockmen of Escalante gradually penetrated the canyon lands bordering the Colorado. Thus, the early stockmen were the discoverers of the lower canyons of the Escalante. They were the first to see the outstanding features of the landscape so much appreciated today—the arches and bridges, the canyons—and

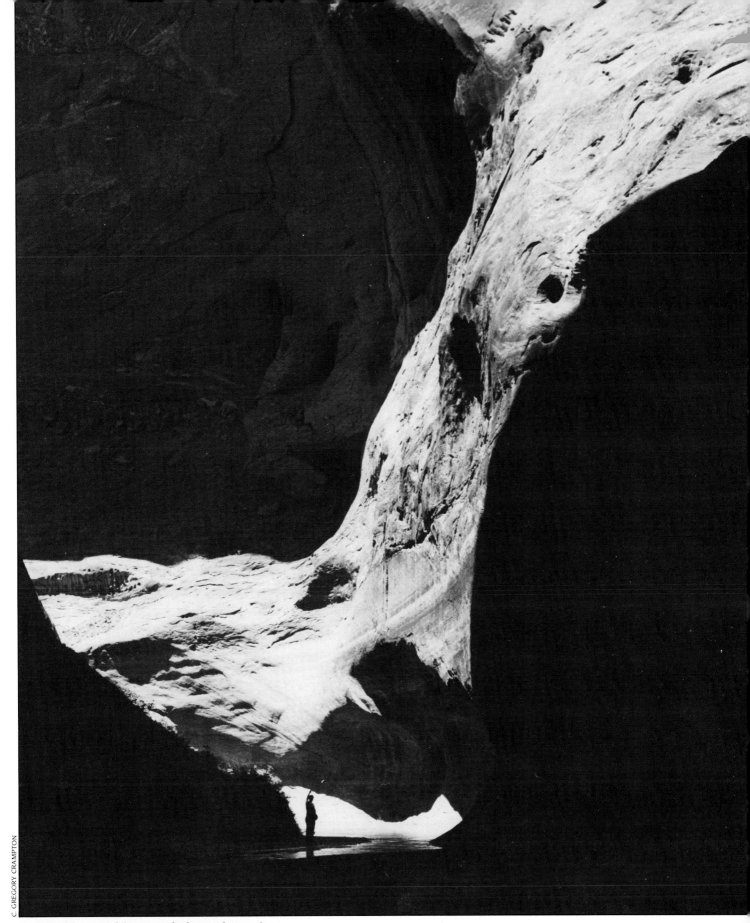

C. GREGORY CRAMPTON

Davis Gulch, named for an early-day cattleman, is one of the deep, tortuous side canyons of the Escalante River. Two of the Escalante Basin's imposing rock arches, as well as prehistoric Indian ruins and rock art, are found here. Everett Ruess camped at a natural corral in the upper part of the canyon before he disappeared. This photo portrays a section of the lower canyon before it was flooded by Lake Powell.

most of these features were named by, or for, them. The stockmen (perhaps we should include here a few rustlers!) opened trails into, out of, and across the canyon.

With the growth of recreational travel before and after World War II, the Escalante canyons were "discovered" again by latter-day explorers, many of whom published their findings.

One of the first in modern times to appreciate and write about the Navajo Country and the canyon wilderness of southern Utah was the youthful and sensitive artist, Everett Ruess. Tramping around the Sierra Nevada, the California coast, and the desert wilderness of the Southwest, Ruess sought beauty in nature with intensity and devotion. He often traveled alone, stopping in small country towns for mail and supplies. In mid-November, 1934, with two burros, Everett left Escalante and headed out over the Hole-in-the-Rock road bound for the canyon country along the Colorado. Not far from the Hole he camped with two sheepherders. He was not seen again. At age 21, Everett Ruess mysteriously disappeared. A search party found his camp and burros in Davis Gulch, a canyon of exceptional beauty and one rich in history. The searchers were able to determine that Ruess had explored some Indian ruins and prehistoric rock art in Davis Gulch, but the young man had vanished. The natural corral in Davis Gulch, where Ruess camped, is about a mile above Lake Powell's high-water mark.

The full story of Everett Ruess, his life and writings and art, and the long effort of his family to solve the mystery of his disappearance, has been told by W.L. Rusho in the book *Everett Ruess, a Vagabond for Beauty* (1983). The book contains a large body of Everett's correspondence, some of his art work and photographs.

Centuries ago, when prehistoric Indians roamed the canyons, the Escalante River was well known to both Anasazi and Fremont peoples. Coming from the east, the Anasazis crossed Glen Canyon and gradually moved up the Escalante to establish a frontier outpost, as it were, deep in Fremont territory. They occupied the Kaiparowits Plateau and, about A.D. 1075, they planted a substantial settlement near the present town of Boulder, Utah. This settlement, now known as the Coombs site, became a cultural mingling ground of two peoples, though it remained predominantly Anasazi in character throughout its two hundred years of existence. The Coombs village was abandoned about A.D. 1275, and the many structures, which had housed as many as 200 people, moldered for nearly 700 years. The site was excavated in the late 1950s, an element in the extensive Glen Canyon archeological salvage project designed to learn the prehistory of the reservoir area before Lake Powell was formed. Although many miles distant from the lake, archeologists believed that they could learn something about the lifestyle of Anasazis living in a large village that would shed light on the human ecology of their cultural relatives in Glen Canyon where there were few large sites. The Coombs village has been partially restored and may be seen in the easily-reached Anasazi Indian Village State Historical Monument at Boulder, Utah.

And what of the Fremont people who also lived in the Escalante basin? They left behind numerous small sites but no large village compounds. But among them were artists of exceptional talent, whose paintings and etchings on rock were seldom rivaled. Examples of their distinctive rock art exist in many places throughout Fremont territory including the Escalante drainage. Go back now to Davis Gulch. Near the stream's confluence with the Escalante River, there is a splendid panel of white pictographs showing shadowy human-like figures along with a number of geometric designs. Unfortunately, the panel is right at the high-water mark of Lake Powell, and the fluctuating lake alternatively exposes and covers the panel subjecting it to the messy deposits found in the "bathtub ring." Everett Ruess saw these paintings before his disappearance in 1934.

C. GREGORY CRAMPTON

C. GREGORY CRAMPTON

Top, a section of the panel of Fremont-style pictographs at Davis Gulch. The prehistoric artist who worked on the four tall figures with trapezoidal bodies (a Fremont hallmark) probably used two different grades of paint. In time, one grade flaked off giving the four an abstract appearance. The figures measure about two feet in height. Above, this remarkable pictograph (enlarged from the panel above) was made by painting in the background, leaving the silhouette blank.

Gregory Natural Bridge spanned (127 feet) Fifty-mile Creek near its confluence with the Escalante River. Cowboys saw it first, and a U.S. Geological Survey mapping crew came in 1921. In July of 1940, Norman Nevills and a boating party in Glen Canyon walked to the bridge. Although other names were suggested, Barry M. Goldwater insisted that the "discovery" should be named after the geologist Herbert E. Gregory. Now that the bridge has been completely covered by the waters of Lake Powell, the name has been transferred to the beautiful butte downstream.

W.L. RUSHO.

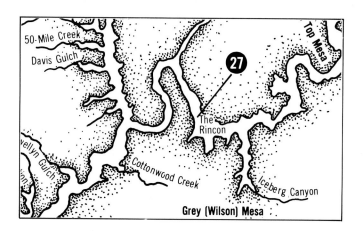

27 Oil Seep Bar

Prospectors wrote one of the longest chapters in Glen Canyon history. The quest for gold, copper, oil, and uranium carried free-roaming types all over the canyon country in pursuit of whatever mineral seemed at the time to offer the greatest promise. Most prospects in Glen Canyon were marginal, and few of them panned out very well since the logistics of mining in such a rugged and difficult environment were too costly. One rugged place was the Rincon (Spanish meaning "corner") about eight miles above the Escalante River, prospected first for gold, then oil, and finally, uranium. There was even a small copper prospect in the vicinity.

The Rincon is an extraordinary example—unique in such dramatic outline in Glen Canyon—of an entrenched meander abandoned when the Colorado cut through the two walls at the neck of a sharp loop. To appreciate the Rincon, it is best seen from the air as in the photograph shown here. Lake Powell was about two-thirds full when this photo was taken in November, 1965. By then most of the mineral prospects in the vicinity had been covered, including the interesting development at Oil Seep Bar.

Just below the Rincon on the right side, several oil seeps had been noticed by travelers as early as 1881, but no extensive exploration took place there until the automobile came of age. As the auto industry burgeoned after World War I, an oil fever swept through the canyon country and a few wells were drilled. Much interest was shown in the Rincon, Waterpocket Fold, and the lower Escalante River. One of several companies interested in the area, the Henry Mountain Oil Company, undertook drilling operations at Oil Seep Bar.

WAYNE B. ALCORN/NATIONAL PARK SERVICE

C. GREGORY CRAMPTON

Aerial view of the Rincon, an ancient, abandoned meander of the Colorado River. Now Lake Powell extends up the channel of the Rincon some distance, but it covers less than half of the loop. Through the decades prospectors scrambled about this rugged place but found no bonanzas. A trickle of crude oil was found at Oil Seep Bar.

Oil in Glen Canyon. River traveler examines petroleum oozing from the rock at Oil Seep Bar where commercial drilling began in 1920.

Under the supervision of Frank Bennett, who had been involved in various gold mining ventures in Glen Canyon since 1897, operations began in July, 1920. Heavy drilling equipment, machinery, lumber, and supplies were floated down the river from Hite and from Hall's Crossing. Some supplies were packed in over rough trails across the Waterpocket Fold. The company drilled four wells at the site, sometimes called Bennett's Oil Field, two in the seep area near the river and two at higher elevations. After much expense and labor the company closed down sometime in 1921. Oil had been found in one of the lower wells but the flow was sluggish—anything but a gusher. On a visit to the site in September, 1960, I dipped crude oil from one of the lower wells. The seeps were still seeping, trapping insects and unwary lizards.

UTAH STATE HISTORICAL SOCIETY

Breakfast on the beach in the "oil field." The caption on this 1921 photograph reads, "Ham and eggs by the shovel full."

R.C. MOORE/U.S. GEOLOGICAL SURVEY

Man on horseback watched oil drilling rig in operation at the upper well, 1921. This spot is very close to the high-water mark of Lake Powell.

C. GREGORY CRAMPTON

The living quarters at Oil Seep were small but cozy. The barrels were empty.

C. GREGORY CRAMPTON

A student of Glen Canyon history takes note of drilling equipment used at Oil Seep Bar in 1920.

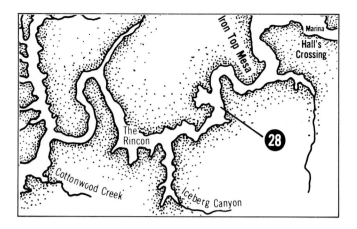

28 Gretchen Bar

Gretchen Bar, also known as Schock Bar, was one of the more productive, gold-bearing localities in Glen Canyon. On this gravel bar, over two miles in length, mining began as early as 1889 and continued intermittently to the 1940s. Of course, we don't know how much gold came out of Gretchen, but judging by the quantity of machinery and equipment left behind when all operations finally ceased, it must have amounted to a considerable sum.

Near a fine spring, a cemented rock cabin was built on the narrow riverbank. Water from the spring was piped to the cabin and was used to irrigate figs, apricots, pomegranates, and grapes planted in the front yard. All manner of interesting relics used by prospectors operating at different times were left scattered over the bar. Gretchen Bar is now entirely covered by Lake Powell.

C. GREGORY CRAMPTON

Late summer camp in 1962, on the left bank a mile and a half below Gretchen Bar.

Complete with fireplace, this solid rock cabin lent the comforts of home to the miners at Gretchen Bar.

Traveler looks over this large monitor, or nozzle, used in hydraulic mining. Water under heavy pressure was forced through the monitor to wash gravel into sluice boxes where the gold, if any, was recovered. There was little evidence on Gretchen Bar of hydraulic mining.

The author "operates" a Model Thirty Caterpillar which had been driven overland from Blanding, Utah, much of the way across slickrock and sand.

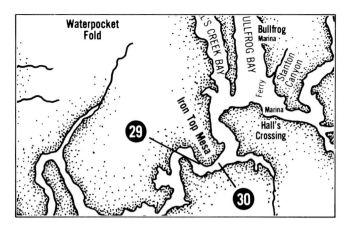

29 Schock Trail

Comparable to the trail to Klondike Bar (See No. 19), Schock Trail is another long and dramatic stock trail which reached the floor of Glen Canyon over slickrock and a series of cutaway steps from Iron Top Mesa, nearly 1,000 feet above the river. The trail, which originates at Baker Ranch (See No. 34), takes its name from one W.H. Schock, a prospector active in Glen Canyon for about 20 years after 1898. For those who knew him, the man was usually called "Dr. Schock." He appears to have been a practitioner of the Thomsonian system of medicine which emphasized hot baths and vegetable and herbal prescriptions. While in the Glen Canyon country he was the only "doctor" available, and he had frequent opportunity to practice. Schock's name is found on location notices a few miles above and below the foot of this trail.

30 Lake Canyon Rapids

In Glen Canyon there were few rapids of any severity, but at the mouth of Lake Canyon there was a rapid of some consequence when the Colorado was low. Here the river flowed over bedrock, the upturned strata of the Waterpocket Fold. During high-water at this point there was nothing more than a gentle ripple, but at low tide the river spread out over a rocky reef making navigation difficult, even hazardous. On one occasion, in September, 1960, my party had to get out and push and lift a rubber boat over the reef!

You don't think of ice in Glen Canyon, but there are records of running ice and of the river being entirely frozen over. When the ice was running it would pile up in shallow places and form jams and ice gorges. In January, 1898, while preparing for his dredging operations upstream (See No. 36), Robert B. Stanton, coming downstream, found an ice jam five feet thick over the rapids below Lake Canyon. While attempting to cut through the jam, a huge field of ice began moving. In "quite a rush" Stanton and party managed to get the boats out before they were jammed to pieces by the ice.

A hiker, resting on a cairn marking the half-way point on the Schock Trail, looks downstream over Iron Rock Island, a gold mining site dating from 1889. Made suitable for pack animals, the trail was marked by a series of picked steps and at one place a dugway 80 feet long had been blasted and picked out of a steep slope. The hiker's position is now 380 feet beneath the surface of Lake Powell.

ROBERT B. STANTON/UNIVERSITY OF UTAH

ROBERT B. STANTON/UNIVERSITY OF UTAH

As the ice in lower Glen Canyon began to move over Lake Canyon Rapids, Robert B. Stanton and company hurried to unload their boats and head for shore, January 3, 1898.

ROBERT B. STANTON/UNIVERSITY OF UTAH

Robert B. Stanton's party chops its way through ice in lower Glen Canyon, January, 1898.

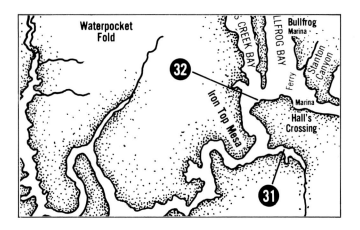

Two history students examine remains of a jigging machine on Boston Bar, a typical gold-mining location in Glen Canyon.

31 Lake Canyon

The name Lake Canyon derives from a half-mile long lake at the head of the canyon some eight miles from the Colorado. Formed behind a dam of wind-blown sand, and kept full by a spring-fed stream, Lake Pagahrit (a Ute name for "Standing Water") was an oasis in a desert wilderness of bare rock, sand, and sparse vegetation. In November, 1915, after three days of heavy rain in the vicinity, the lake overflowed and quickly cut a channel in the sandy dam, causing the impounded waters to thunder down the canyon to the Colorado.

For the Anasazi peoples the lake and the lacustrine vegetation were important resources. This helps explain the fact that Lake Canyon was one of the most heavily used of the Glen Canyon tributaries during prehistoric times. Of the many masonry sites located in the canyon, Wasp House, 1¼ miles from the Colorado, was the most interesting. Lake Powell has filled Lake Canyon to its rims but does not extend to the site of Lake Pagahrit.

32 Boston Bar

Boston Bar, just below Hall's Crossing, was a typical Glen Canyon gold prospect. The rock bench 45 feet above the river was capped with gold-bearing gravel. Using a jigging machine, the remains of which are shown in the photograph, the coarse gravel was screened out. The finer material was chuted down to the river terrace where it was washed through sluice boxes with water pumped from the Colorado. The name comes from the Boston Placer Mining Company which started up mining operations here late in 1899. Many of the post World War II river trippers stopped at Boston Bar, not to study the mining relics, but to view the Great Blue herons nesting in the trees across the river.

C. GREGORY CRAMPTON

Beneath a tapestry wall, Wasp House in Glen Canyon was a popular tourist attraction during the years before the dam.

F.B. SLOTE/BUREAU OF RECLAMATION

A tourist in Lake Canyon walks on bedrock swept clean by rushing water when the blowsand dam at Lake Pagahrit gave way in November, 1915.

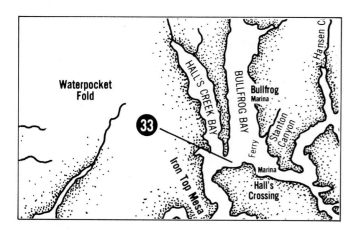

33 Hall's Crossing

Hall's Crossing was opened in 1881 by Charles Hall as a substitute for the precarious crossing at Hole-in-the-Rock (See No. 24). A skilled carpenter, Hall had built the ferryboat at Hole-in-the-Rock, and he remained there through 1880, but few people crossed since the approach roads were too steep, rough, and hazardous. Hall scouted for a better crossing and found one 35 miles upstream, a short distance above the mouth of Hall's Creek.

At the new location the approach roads were better. Travelers coming from the west had to cross the Circle Cliffs and the Waterpocket Fold, but upon reaching Hall's Creek the going was fairly easy. Near the river the road dropped down over a sloping slickrock bench to reach the ferry site. On the east the road crossed open sand and slickrock country to reach the rim of Glen Canyon opposite the mouth of Bullfrog Creek. Then it dropped down over gravel and bare rock benches to the riverbank.

For a ferry, Charles Hall brought logs, planks, and pitch from Escalante and built a crude boat 30 feet long and tapered at each end. There was no cable or rope to guide the craft. It was towed upstream and then shoved off with the payload. One man steered and two rowed as the ferry floated downstream, angling under the two-man power toward the opposite bank. On the return trip the boat was towed upstream and then rowed across on a downstream slant to the opposite bank. Ferry charges were usually about $5.00 per wagon and $.75 for each horse.

Charles Hall put the ferry in operation in 1881, but there weren't very many customers and he went out of business in 1884. The completion of the Denver-Rio Grande Western Railroad across north central Utah in 1883 and the increased use of the Lee's Ferry route between Utah and Arizona reduced the isolation of the frontier folk in southeastern Utah and made the long, rough trek across the canyons an experience to be avoided.

The ferry business was only the first paragraph in the history of the crossing. By the time Charles Hall left, the gold rush was beginning in Glen Canyon, and the crossing became a major gateway for prospectors moving up and down the river. It is frequently mentioned in location notices and in the mining literature of the canyon. A documentary of this activity was found on the right bank on a cliff face, shaded from the afternoon sun. There was a register of many names inscribed on the rock by those who had camped there for a day or two or longer. Some of the inscriptions were done with care and are deserving of remembrance.

In recent times, the sandy beach and shady bank at Hall's Crossing became one of the camping spots in Glen Canyon most enjoyed by recreational boaters.

And now a motorized ferryboat runs between two lakeside marinas at this historic crossing. Charles Hall could scarcely have imagined as much.

W.L. RUSHO

LILLIE HALL DENNY

Top, campers under the willows at Hall's Crossing waiting for breakfast. Above, Charles Hall, pioneer ferryman at Hole-in-the-Rock and Hall's Crossing.

Man with camera walks down eastern approach road to Hall's Crossing. The Colorado River flowed from right to left. The ferry operated between the white sandbar and the brush-covered bar on the opposite side. The road and the entire crossing area is now beneath Lake Powell.

Billy Bright and Jack Butler were gold prospectors who spent 12 years in Glen Canyon.

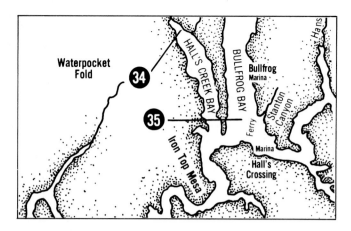

34 Baker Ranch

Within the Lake Powell reservoir area there were few places of any size put under cultivation in historic times. Baker Ranch, six miles from Hall's Crossing, was one of the largest of these. At one time approximately 100 acres of alfalfa and corn were irrigated by water diverted from Hall's Creek. Between 1907 and the 1940s the Thomas Smith family, and later, Eugene Baker and sons, founded and operated a desert ranch now underwater near the head of Hall's Creek embayment of Lake Powell.

Some years ago Carlyle Baker, son of Eugene Baker, told me about life on the ranch. During the spring, when storms broke over the Waterpocket Fold, enough water came down Hall's Creek to irrigate many acres. However, grazing, not farming, was the main business at the ranch. But there were uncertainties—erratic water supply, hot climate of the summer months, sandy soil—and the Bakers finally sold the property.

During the years between the two world wars the ranch was a single habitation in the wilderness. Though it was remote and lonely, it still figured in the life of the central Glen Canyon region. It was a terminal point for a trail crossing the Waterpocket Fold and the Lower Escalante River; it was a supply point for some of the Glen Canyon mining camps reached by way of the Schock Trail (See No. 29); it was a way point on the road to Hall's Crossing.

How ironic that the desert ranch died by drowning!

35 Bullfrog

Bullfrog Creek, a long tributary of the Colorado, heads in the Henry Mountains, flows through an open valley much of the way, and entered the river through a shallow canyon. The great fan of boulders at the mouth of the creek generated a well-known stretch of fast water where the Colorado dropped about four feet in half a mile. When the river was up, waves three to four feet high gave boaters a choppy ride through one of the few rapids in Glen Canyon. The name Bullfrog Rapids was in use in 1899 during the mining period in Glen Canyon, and it appears that the creek was named after the rapids. For many years the stream was known as Pine Alcove Creek, a name given by the Wheeler Survey in 1873 and used on the early maps past the turn of the century. It is quite likely that the present usage was fixed when Bullfrog Creek appeared on the river maps published by the U.S. Geological Survey in 1922.

C. GREGORY CRAMPTON

September, 1960. A river boatman looks across the Colorado to the mouth of Bullfrog Creek and the wide valley beyond now covered by Lake Powell and Bullfrog Bay. When this photo was made, the river was very low. The huge fan of boulders and debris deflected the river to the left side where it flowed close to the bank and was scarcely visible from the photographer's standpoint. The boatman is standing near the place where Hall's Crossing Marina was built.

C. GREGORY CRAMPTON

A visitor examines the main house at the *Baker Ranch. The cliffs of Hall Mesa in the background rise nearly 500 feet above the building complex.*

A boating party heads downstream on a wide reach of the Colorado River a few miles below Hite.

W. L. RUSHO

SECTION IV

BULLFROG AND HALL'S CROSSING TO HITE

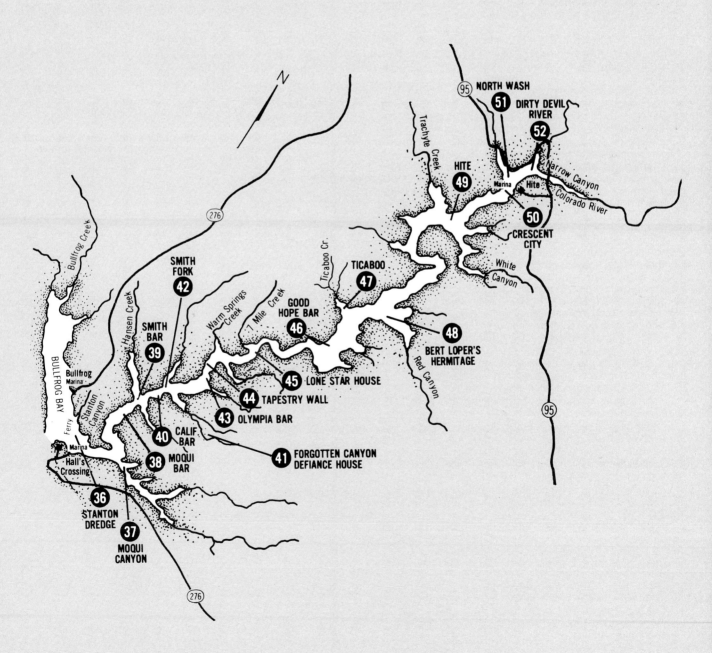

N

95 NORTH WASH
51
DIRTY DEVIL RIVER
52

Trachyte Creek

HITE
49

Narrow Canyon

Marina

Hite

Colorado River

50

CRESCENT CITY

276

White Canyon

Bullfrog Creek

SMITH FORK
42

Warm Springs Creek

Ticaboo Cr.

TICABOO
47

7 Mile Creek

GOOD HOPE BAR
46

Hansen Creek

SMITH BAR
39

48
BERT LOPER'S HERMITAGE

Red Canyon

BULLFROG BAY

Bullfrog Marina

45 LONE STAR HOUSE

44 TAPESTRY WALL

Stanton Canyon

43 OLYMPIA BAR

Ferry

40 CALIF BAR

38 MOQUI BAR

41 FORGOTTEN CANYON DEFIANCE HOUSE

Marina

Hall's Crossing

36

STANTON DREDGE

37

MOQUI CANYON

276

95

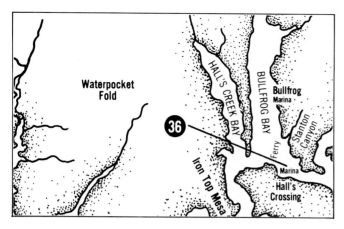

ROBERT B. STANTON/UNIVERSITY OF UTAH

36 The Stanton Gold Dredge

The biggest mining enterprise in Glen Canyon was undertaken on behalf of the Hoskaninni Company by the bold and imaginative engineer, Robert Brewster Stanton. Operations dated from 1897 to 1901 and centered on the right bank of the river 2.5 miles above Bullfrog Creek, where the company installed a massive gold dredge. The venture was a financial failure, and the rusting dredge, visible in the river until it was covered by Lake Powell, stood as a monument to man's quest for gold.

While running a railroad survey through the canyons of the Colorado, Stanton had become interested in the mining possibilities in Glen Canyon. Having made two trips through Glen in 1889, when the gold rush was in full swing, he had seen many prospectors at work. Coming back as engineer and field superintendent for the Hoskaninni Company, Stanton determined that dredging would be the best way to extract gold from the Glen Canyon sand and gravel. He planned to start with one dredge; if it were successful others would be built and installed at separate places in the canyon. The site chosen for the pilot project was named Camp Stone after Julius F. Stone, president of the company.

Before the dredge began operating early in 1901, Camp Stone was humming with activity. Men and horses, machinery, equipment, and supplies were all brought to the site. Tent houses were set up, a mess hall, ice plant, and blacksmith shop were built. The assembling and construction of the huge dredge was a colossal job. From the railhead at Green River, Utah, over a hundred miles away, the machinery and equipment were hauled in wagons to the rim of Glen Canyon. In order for teams and wagons to reach the river, a steep dugway was blasted out of the side of a short canyon, since named Stanton Canyon. Once on the riverbank, all freight was transported by boats of various kinds upstream one mile to Camp Stone where the dredge was assembled.

Gold dredging is a form of placer mining, that is, the recovery of the mineral in its free state from alluvial matter. The Hoskaninni dredge was equipped with 46 buckets fastened to an endless chain which ran on a ladder. Sand and gravel from the river were brought up in the buckets and dumped automatically on to a rotating, cylindrical, coarse, steel screen. Material passing through the screen was carried over amalgamating tables coated with mercury. Waste was returned to the river and the amalgam was distilled in a retort to obtain the free gold.

With the dredge completed early in 1901, Robert B. Stanton began operations in the riverbed adjacent to Camp Stone. But the dredge failed, mainly because the sluicing and amalgamating machinery did not save the gold. Stanton reported a cleanup of $30.15 on April 13, and another of $36.80 on May 7, 1901, a meager return on an investment probably in excess of $100,000! Colorado River gold was very fine—it was literally gold dust—which thwarted the best efforts of most Glen Canyon prospectors. Coarse gold was seldom found.

C. GREGORY CRAMPTON

Top, workman at entrance to the main tent house at Camp Stone. Above, in 1963 a traveler observes that only the fireplace remains of the same tent house.

ROBERT B. STANTON/UNIVERSITY OF UTAH

The Stanton gold dredge completed and in operation.

ROBERT B. STANTON/UNIVERSITY OF UTAH

*Under the flying flag workmen construct
the hull on ways and then slide it down to
the river...*

ROBERT B. STANTON/UNIVERSITY OF UTAH

*...where machinery and superstructure
are added.*

81

The dredge was nearly a complete loss; nothing much was salvaged. Parts of the dredge, and the supplies and equipment left at Camp Stone were appropriated by miners; pieces of machinery were removed and some of the lumber was stripped off to make rafts and miner's shacks downstream. On a river trip in 1909, Julius F. Stone, the Hoskaninni Company's president, photographed the dredge as it looked then. On another trip in 1938, Stone told his companions that he had invested heavily in the Hoskaninni Company but had received nothing in return. In order to save Stone from a total loss, the party stopped at the dredge and removed enough lumber to build a fire that evening. A pot of coffee was boiled and Stone drank a cup. "This is the only return I ever had from the Hoskaninni investment," Stone said. "This cup of coffee cost me $5,000."

In 1902 the dredge had been moved downstream to a point opposite the mouth of Stanton Canyon where the massive relic was viewed by many river parties until it was covered by Lake Powell whose waters at this point are now 335 feet deep. The lower part of Stanton Canyon and the steep dugway down to the river are also covered.

A final note: As part of the assessment work carried out by the Hoskaninni Company, Stanton made a number of "improvements" at Hole-in-the-Rock (See No. 24), Lee's Ferry (See No. 66), and other places.

C. GREGORY CRAMPTON

A river runner examines the remains of the Hoskaninni gold dredge.

JULIUS F. STONE/GRAND CANYON NATIONAL PARK

When Julius F. Stone saw the dredge in 1909, it was beginning to give in to the power of the river.

ROBERT B. STANTON/UNIVERSITY OF UTAH

Freighters head down the dugway in Stanton Canyon.

CHARLES KELLY/UTAH STATE HISTORICAL SOCIETY

ROBERT B. STANTON/UNIVERSITY OF UTAH

*Freighters hauling dredging equipment wait at the head of
Stanton Canyon for the signal to descend the steep dugway
down to the river.*

*Julius Stone enjoys a slice of watermelon
as he contemplates a $5,000 cup of coffee
brewing on the fire built of timber from
the Hoskaninni dredge.*

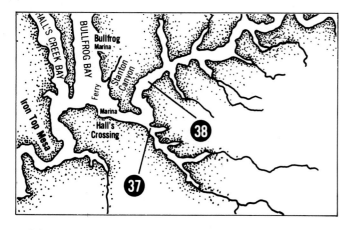

37 Moqui Canyon

The history of Moqui (also Moki) Canyon has been written mainly by archeologists who discovered that the canyon held abundant evidence of heavy usage by prehistoric people. Remains of the Basketmakers, dating back to A.D. 500, have been found here. Moqui, a Hopi word meaning "dead," was commonly used in Glen Canyon and elsewhere in the Southwest to describe almost anything that looked like it had been made by prehistoric man. Thus, in Glen Canyon there were Moqui ruins (See No. 49, paragraph on Fort Moqui), pottery, steps, petroglyphs, etc. There was a Moqui Bar (See No. 38), and here, a canyon where prehistoric remains were found in some quantity.

Moqui Canyon heads in the Clay Hills and Mancos Mesa and reached the Colorado through a deeply-incised canyon. The canyon offered just the right combination of resources to appeal to the ancient ones, and they made the most of them. So many of their buildings, here and elsewhere in the canyon country, were placed in striking locations. I like to think that in picking a place to build they considered the view as well as the water supply.

It is probable that the first white men to explore the canyon were prospectors who worked their way up from the river. We can safely say that they found no gold, but they did see the several cliff-side ruins tucked away in sheltering alcoves. And it was likely they who coined the name and reported the prehistoric ruins.

Now, one of the avowed searchers after ruins of the time was Clayton Wetherill, one of the brothers of the well-known Wetherill family, who arrived in Moqui Canyon in 1897 only to find that other "searchers" before him had emptied the ruins of artifacts. An article by Neil Judd, reporting a National Geographic Society expedition in 1923, brought some of the canyon's archeological riches and scenic beauties before a wide-reading audience. In 1929, Charles L. Bernheimer and Earl H. Morris visited Moqui Canyon on an archeological expedition. In the 1930s and 1940s as recreational boating began to develop in Glen Canyon, Moqui Canyon was one of the more frequented places. Before the dam was built, the University of Utah Department of Anthropology made a thorough scientific and salvage study of the historic canyon.

38 Moqui Bar

This was one of the richer gold mining bars in Glen Canyon. Over a mile long, a sandy terrace was backed up by gravel capped benches at the base of cliffs ranging from 75 to 100 feet high. Of course, it was the ancient Ice Age gravels that produced most of the gold in Glen Canyon. Overland access to the bar was by way of a stock trail built over a prehistoric route of pecked ("Moqui") steps, which to the prospectors probably suggested the name Moqui Bar. The site is entirely covered by Lake Powell.

Top, river runners hike up Moqui Canyon, and, above, climb to reach prehistoric ruins in an alcove.

C. GREGORY CRAMPTON

Modern explorers climb the trail to Moqui Bar. Two lower figures follow ancient pecked steps visible above them and near upper figure who stands on a picked trail used by miners.

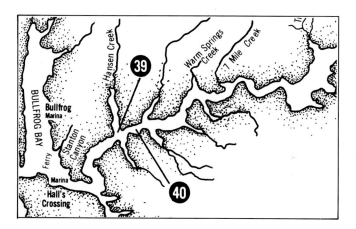

39 Hansen Creek/ Smith Bar

Hansen Creek is important historically mainly because it was an access route into Glen Canyon from the west serving Smith Bar at the mouth of the canyon, Moqui Bar (See No. 37), and California Bar (See No. 40) across the river. The canyon of Hansen Creek was one of the few Glen Canyon tributaries passable by wagons, and a road of sorts was opened through it in the 1890s.

Smith Bar, sometimes known as Smith Brothers Bar, was a mile-long sand and gravel terrace bisected by Hansen Creek. Placer mining at the upper end of the bar was in progress when the Stanton expedition stopped there in December, 1889. Learning of the gold mining in Glen Canyon, Stanton returned later to launch the Hoskaninni venture (See No. 36).

40 California Bar

Near the center of the mile-long California Bar was a gold deposit which was probably one of the richest in Glen Canyon. During his work on the Hoskaninni venture, Robert B. Stanton reported that $30,000 had been taken out of these diggings before 1899. Abandoned mining equipment scattered about told the story of the gold hunters who worked the bar intermittently until the mid-1940s. Little is known about Alonzo G. Turner who prospected here and there in Glen Canyon and in Cataract Canyon. He spent some time at California Bar and never left it.

Centuries before the white man arrived, prehistoric Indians reached the bar over a steep trail of pecked steps, enlarged with picks by miners in recent times.

Lake Powell at California Bar is 338 feet deep.

Anasazi trail to California Bar.

Mining machinery at the "Smith Bros. Placers" at the upper end of Smith Bar. Photograph was made by the Stanton railroad survey expedition in December, 1889. Across the river is the lower end of California Bar and the mouth of Crystal Springs Canyon, and farther downstream on the left is the upper end of Moqui Bar.

86

Hikers reach the head of California Bar, reported to be one of the richest placer mines in Glen Canyon.

C. GREGORY CRAMPTON

C. GREGORY CRAMPTON

On April 23, 1923, Alonzo Turner died at California Bar. His comrades erected a hand-mixed, hand-inscribed concrete gravestone. Once the misspelling was noted, it was too late to back up.

Field researcher attempts to describe this sluice box, gravel chute, and ladder at California Bar.

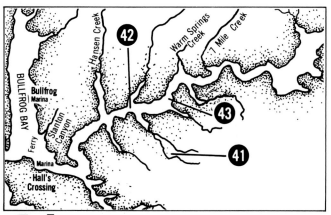

41 Forgotten Canyon/ Defiance House

Some time after 1922 a party of river runners discovered that this canyon, a major Glen Canyon tributary, had been omitted from the U.S. Geological Survey's river map published in that year. On the spot the party promptly named it "Forgotten Canyon."

In terms of human history the canyon should be remembered primarily for its archeological wealth. One of the best of the remains left behind by the ancient Anasazis— Defiance House—is above the water and has been restored. Here was a pueblo with a kiva (ceremonial room), three dwelling areas, four storage rooms, and two enclosed work areas. The pueblo was occupied for about 200 years, A.D. 1100–1300.

Archeologists who studied the pueblo said the name Defiance House was suggested by its sheltered position, by a low rock wall protecting the front, and especially, by three warlike human figures brandishing clubs and circular shields painted on the wall above the structures. Note that two of the figures hold the club in the right hand and the shield in the left, while the third figure is left-handed. This striking panel, possibly unique in Glen Canyon, is clearly visible from the lake.

42 Smith Fork

A stream heading on Mt. Ellsworth in the Henry Mountains, Smith Fork divided a mile-long sandy riverbar occupied by Anasazis from about A.D. 1050 to 1300. The Indians farmed the sandy flats near the river, and when not in the fields, they decorated the nearby cliffs with petroglyphs creating over the years one of the richest panels of rock art in Glen Canyon.

In the 1880s gold prospectors tried their luck on the bar at Smith Fork, but the returns were probably meager if we may judge by the following inscription left by one who arrived at a later date:

"P. DeVries   17 March 1912 N. Holland
Europa thought he was going to get rich
in the USA but did not"

The inscription undoubtedly sums up the experience of many a gold seeker in Glen Canyon.

43 Olympia Bar

Olympia Bar was a left bank gold mining site and one of dramatic proportions. Gold in small quantities was found in a series of gravel-covered terraces, the highest being about 200 feet above the Colorado. Mining began in 1897 and was carried on at all the terrace levels. Through the use of scrapers, ore cars, chutes, and shovels great quantities of gravel were dumped and otherwise moved down to near the level of the river where a wheel lifted water for sluicing operations. Perched on a ledge overlooking the river, the water wheel, held in place by pieces of cable and put together with driftwood lumber and other available materials, was a masterpiece of ingenuity. We have no production statistics for Olympia, but like nearly all of the diggings in Glen Canyon, the gold here was too fine to save.

Top, the gladiators of Defiance House. The figure on the right is about four feet tall. Middle, a hunting scene among the petroglyphs at Smith Fork. Bighorn sheep are common in prehistoric rock art, but hunting pictorials are rare. Above, Anasazi art gallery at Smith Fork.

W.L. RUSHO

Remains of the water wheel at Olympia Bar as it appeared in May, 1963. Even though the cables were floppy and loose, the frame still stood.

C. GREGORY CRAMPTON

Modern explorers are dwarfed by a great pile of gravel at Olympia Bar.

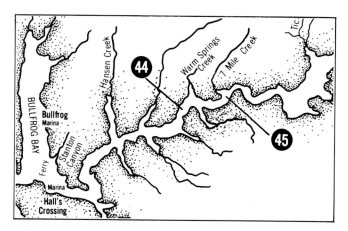

44 Tapestry Wall

Opposite the head of Olympia Bar and just below the mouth of Warm Springs Creek is Tapestry Wall. This magnificent mile-long curving cliff stood, in one place, an even thousand feet above the Colorado. On a bend in the river it could be seen for over two miles up- or downstream. In use as early as 1897, the name comes from the "tapestry" effect created by sediment-laden water running down the face of the cliff. The black-on-red in vertical streaks is commonly seen on Glen Canyon cliffs of which this is a superb example. At its highest point Tapestry Wall stands 685 feet above the surface of Lake Powell.

The Tapestry Wall area was a great place to camp. On my trips we worked out a schedule like this: Stop at Warm Springs Creek for fresh water. (There were no warm springs but there was always a good flow of cool spring water near the mouth.) Then, cross the river to camp on the upper end of Olympia Bar. There, opposite the great wall facing east across the river, we would watch the rising sun illuminate the tapestry from top to bottom. On one September evening we were nearly blown off the beach as a summer storm moved in. Sand got into everything including the camera lens!

45 Lone Star House

Opposite the mouth of Sevenmile Creek stood a rock house occupied from time to time by prospectors working claims between Olympia Bar and Good Hope Bar six miles upstream. In 1897, Robert B. Stanton referred to the building as "O'Keefe's Lone Star Rock House," but other sources refer to it as the Ryan cabin. Both Timothy O'Keefe and M.J. "Mike" Ryan are names appearing on local mining notices in the 1890s. This was no miner's shack. It was a large one-room building about 14 feet square on the inside. The walls and the fireplace were built of sandstone slabs; a ridgepole between gabled ends supported a brush and dirt covered roof. The two windows and the front door facing the river were set in frames. A four-pointed star had been etched on a big rock near the house.

Campers engulfed by a sand blow on the beach opposite Tapestry Wall.

A camper admires a section of Tapestry Wall where it towers a thousand feet above the river.

C. GREGORY CRAMPTON

A river traveler looks over the Lone Star House, a Glen Canyon "showpiece."

C. GREGORY CRAMPTON

On one hot August day the author's party stopped for water at Warm Springs Canyon. The view is downstream across the Colorado to the opposite bank. Little power was used in Glen Canyon: the outboard is a 3-horsepower, air-cooled model, enough to steer the seven-man neoprene raft.

C. GREGORY CRAMPTON

91

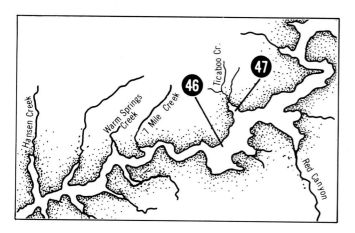

46 Good Hope Bar

Good Hope Bar was an extensive sand and gravel bar on the inside of an elbow bend on the right bank of the Colorado. It figured prominently in the gold placer mining history of Glen Canyon as the location of a number of ventures. Gold was discovered here in 1887 and much mining took place on the bar. In 1902, the Good Hope Placer Mining Company received a federal patent, that is, title, to four of its claims. An interesting aspect of the operations here was that the owners built a water wheel at the river's edge and a flume 700 feet long to carry the water to the mining site.

47 Ticaboo

A creek by this name heads on the eastern slopes of Mt. Ellsworth, one of the Henry Mountains. It reached the Colorado River near the center of a series of low, gravel-covered benches where Cass Hite and others discovered gold in 1885. Indeed the area is to be identified with Hite, who spent much of his life here after he arrived in Glen Canyon in 1883 (See No. 49.). The name Ticaboo was applied to the placer claims by Cass, who said it was a Navajo word meaning "friend." The name was also given to the creek and to a set of light rapids where the creek entered the river.

Walking over the gravel bars, as I did a number of times, one could see much evidence of placer mining. At one point right on the riverbank a crude one-room cabin had been built of assorted pieces of driftwood. This was near the place Hite called the "Bank of Ticaboo," since, as he said, he had a lot of gold on deposit there. Hite was active in promoting his placer prospects in Glen Canyon, and the Bank of Ticaboo was a good place to show prospective clients the values to be obtained from Colorado River gravels. He appears to have been a strong believer in the idea that it is easier to mine gold out of investors' pockets than out of the ground. During the railroad survey, Robert B. Stanton stopped here twice in 1889 at a time when Hite was actively at work in the Ticaboo diggings. What the engineer saw here and elsewhere in Glen Canyon suggested the idea of a gold dredging project (See No. 36).

Along Ticaboo Creek, about a mile from the Colorado, Cass Hite built a house where he lived much of the time he was in Glen Canyon. With water brought from the creek, he irrigated a garden plot and a vineyard. In 1914, he died at his place and was buried there.

ROBERT B. STANTON/ UNIVERSITY OF UTAH

F. A. NIMS/ENGINEERING SOCIETIES LIBRARY, NEW YORK

Cass Hite's "Bank of Ticaboo." Photo by the Stanton railroad survey, December, 1889.

C. GREGORY CRAMPTON

A view across the Colorado to Good Hope Bar, January 1898. Part of the water wheel and the long flume appear at extreme right, center.

A hiker views the remains of Cass Hite's home on the Ticaboo.

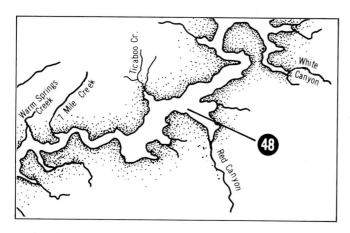

48 Bert Loper's Hermitage

Bert Loper's Hermitage was located near the mouth of Red Canyon, a long tributary of the Colorado heading to the southeast in the Red House Cliffs. As the name suggests, vivid red rock is exposed throughout the canyon, which is generally open and accessible to automobiles of sufficient stamina and clearance. Some two miles upstream from the mouth of Red Canyon stands Castle Butte. It was known to all Glen Canyon river runners and it is still an imposing landmark on Lake Powell.

Although the name of Albert "Bert" Loper, well-known river man, is prominently identified with this area, human history dates back about 800 years to a time when a few Anasazis families moved here to try their luck at farming. On a bluff overlooking the river, the Indians constructed a small two-story pueblo of 11 or 12 rooms flanking a large pit house or kiva. About A.D. 1250, after some 75 years of life on the Colorado, the ancient ones abandoned their village and it fell into ruins. From the river the remains stood out prominently on the skyline, and through the years, centuries later, they attracted many visitors beginning with the Powell expedition in 1869. Before the formation of Lake Powell, University of Utah archeologists made a systematic study of the site, naming it Loper Ruin.

On the gravel-covered benches not far from the Loper Ruin, gold was discovered on Castle Butte Bar as early as 1885. Between 1909 and 1915, Bert Loper, who had already been in the San Juan River gold rush in the 1890s, labored in these diggings. During this time he lived alone in an attractive cabin built of square hewn logs shaded by cottonwoods, a place he called the "hermitage." Shortly after his nearest neighbor Cass Hite died, Bert Loper left his home on the Colorado. But he returned to the river many times, his last in 1949 when, on his eightieth birthday, he lost his life to the Colorado in Grand Canyon (See No. 4). Through his activities on the river during his later years, Loper did much to stimulate recreational travel in Glen Canyon. Many river trippers stopped to see the "Hermitage" and the Loper Ruin (a short hike upstream), until the advancing waters of Lake Powell swallowed them.

Top, still a prominent landmark, Castle Butte stands 770 feet above the surface of Lake Powell. The photo was taken from a point directly over the Loper place where the water is 285 feet deep. Above, a visitor in 1950 pokes around in the Loper Ruin abandoned by the Anasazi Indians about 700 years earlier.

Bert Loper's Hermitage.

W.L. RUSHO

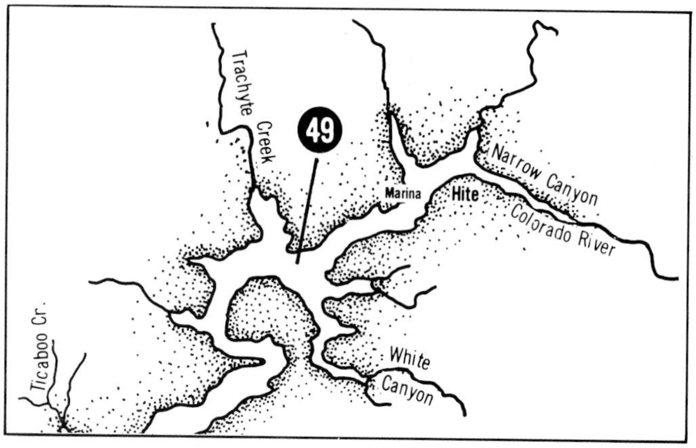

49 Hite

The largest settlement in the entire area covered by Lake Powell was "Hite City," located on the right bank of the Colorado now at a point about five miles downlake from the Hite Marina. The white man's history of settlement in Glen Canyon began in September, 1883, when Cass Hite, who had been prospecting in the Navajo Mountain country, arrived in company with the Navajo Chief Hoskininni. The chief had said that there was gold along the Colorado. He was right. The prospector found gold in the sands and gravels near the place soon to be named Hite. It was these discoveries that set off the Glen Canyon gold rush.

Hite had reached the river by way of White Canyon. Near its mouth he found a good place to cross the Colorado and named it Dandy Crossing. Easily reached from the east by White Canyon and from the west by Trachyte Creek and North Wash, Dandy Crossing was a good one, indeed it was the best in Glen Canyon.

It's called a gold rush. It was slow at first, but as new discoveries were reported the boom took on sizeable proportions. Nearly everyone hoping to strike it rich headed for Hite. It was a jumping-off place for the rushers, who worked their way downstream looking for profitable diggings. Cass Hite put up the first structure, a cabin of notched logs salvaged from the river. The building, used for many purposes, stood through the years until it was swallowed by the rising waters of Lake Powell in July, 1964. As the rush gained momentum, some of Cass Hite's relatives followed him into the canyon—brothers John P. and Ben R., and the latter's son, Homer J. A post office was established at Hite in 1889 and it stayed open until 1914, the year Cass Hite died at his ranch at Ticaboo. The mail was brought by horseback from the railhead at Green River, over 100 miles away. The Hites operated a small store in conjunction with the post office, services much appreciated by local miners and others passing through.

Save for the oil boom, the years after World War I were quiet in Glen Canyon, but with the onset of the Great Depression there was a revival in gold prospecting. Arthur L. Chaffin, who had mined for gold around the turn of the century, came back during the depression. After prospecting for a time, he bought up the properties at Hite and began to develop them extensively. In the age of the automobile Chaffin hoped to open Glen Canyon to the general public.

Cass Hite may have found it to be a "Dandy Crossing," but some others did not. For some time after Hite's arrival in 1883, there were no boats on hand for the convenience of travelers. Dandy Crossing was not a ford. Most of those who crossed in the horse and wagon days had to swim their animals. In a book published in 1906, T. Mitchell Prudden tells of the trials his party had crossing the river. Coming from the east by way of White Canyon, he arrived at the crossing and fired a shot to attract the attention of those on the other side. Three figures appeared and yelled, "What ye want?"

"We want to get across; send over the boat."

E.C. LARUE/U.S. GEOLOGICAL SURVEY

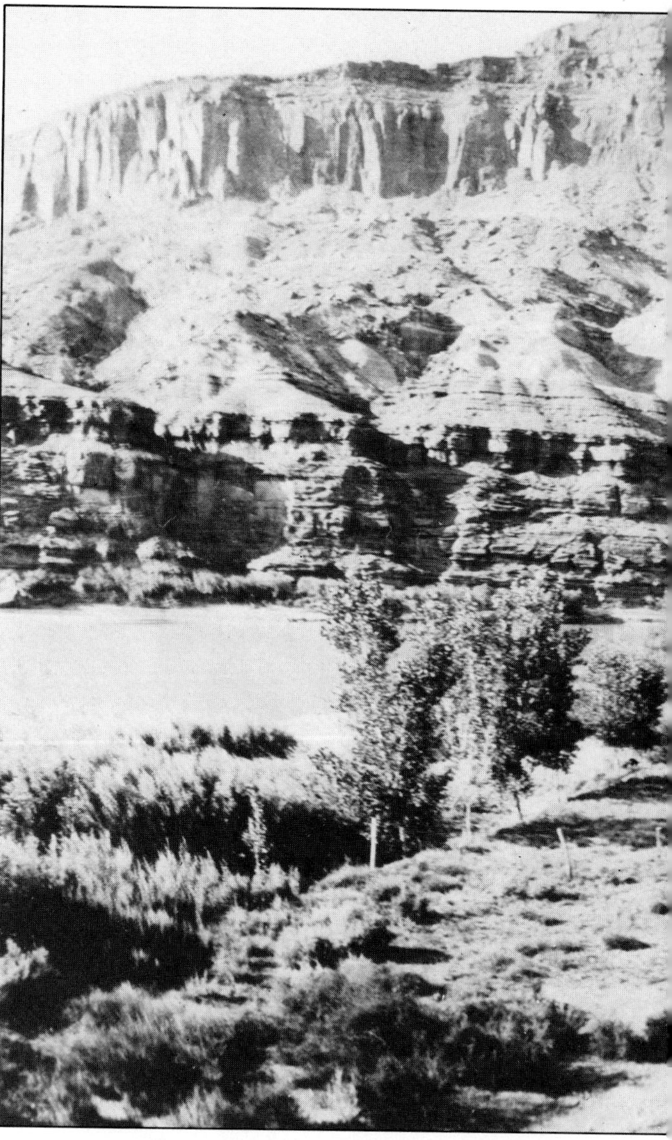

WILLIAM E. RICE

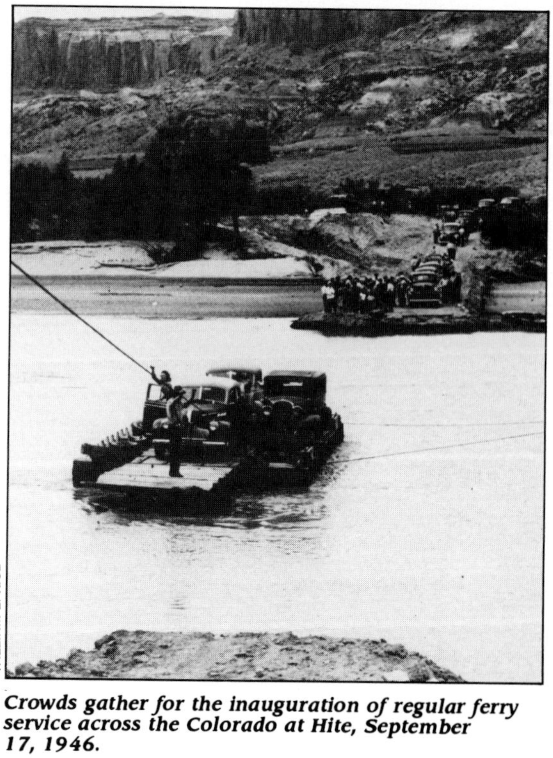

Crowds gather for the inauguration of regular ferry service across the Colorado at Hite, September 17, 1946.

Hite City as it appeared in 1915. It hadn't grown much since Cass Hite arrived on the spot in 1883, but above Lee's Ferry it was the largest settlement on the Glen Canyon frontier.

W. L. RUSHO

The last run of the Chaffin Ferry at Hite on June 5, 1964. View is from Hite on the west bank.

"They ain't no boat; ye can't git over."

Upstream a few miles the Prudden party found a leaky boat. With it, they managed to get themselves and their gear across and tow the cantankerous mules.

Dandy Crossing was a favorite of the outlaws. The approaches were easy. You could ride a horse, or drive a whole herd of horses, right down to the river on either side. And after the beginning of the Glen Canyon gold rush, you could get supplies at Hite, and there was little likelihood of running into the law.

At Hite the horse and wagon days lasted well into the 20th century. It was not until 1946 that a fair dirt road was completed across the canyon country between Hanksville and Blanding, Utah, by way of North Wash and White Canyon. The formal dedication of the road and the inauguration of regular ferry service took place at Hite, September 17, 1946. Over 400 people were in attendance to witness the formal completion of the first satisfactory crossing of Glen Canyon above Lee's Ferry.

The opening of this route was the work of citizens living in the terminal towns, Utah state agencies, and particularly, of Arthur L. Chaffin, resident at Hite since 1932. Before World War II Chaffin had seen firsthand the growing recreational interest in the river and the canyon. Before 1946 he had managed to open a road of sorts following the wagon track up North Wash, and he had even put a crude ferry in operation. Chaffin also built the 1946 ferry, a pontoon craft, ingeniously powered by an automobile engine, which pulled itself across the river guided by a cable. Some of the equipment used to construct the ferry had been brought up from mining sites down the river. The tightener for the pull cable on the ferry had originally been the bull wheel on the drilling rig at Oil Seep Bar (See No. 27). Although it was remodeled a number of times, the ferry, informally known as the Chaffin Ferry, remained in operation until June 5, 1964, when it was taken out of service as Lake Powell encroached on the site. At maximum level, Lake Powell at the ferry site is 255 feet deep.

The historic ferry, the last to run on the Upper Colorado, was used extensively during the canyon country uranium boom of the 1950s and especially during the operation of the uranium mill at the mouth of White Canyon (across the river from Hite).

At the beginning of the uranium boom the Vanadium Corporation of America and the Atomic Energy Commission built an experimental mill for the reduction of uranium ore, which began operating in 1949. The mill was a considerable stimulus to uranium prospecting in Glen Canyon. A small boom camp sprang up on the upstream side of White Canyon. A post office, White Canyon, was established and a one-room schoolhouse for 30 pupils was built. But the mill shut down in mid-1954 and White Canyon quickly became a ghost. The post office, operated by postmaster G.W. Edgell (who also ran the Hite ferry), was moved two miles away to Farley's Canyon. As the rising waters of Lake Powell approached, White Canyon Post Office was discontinued in 1964.

Of course, prehistoric man lived in the Hite area centuries before the coming of the white men. The first whites saw evidence of the early people in many forms: petroglyphs, broken pottery, chipped stone, fallen walls. The most imposing prehistoric structure stood on a prominent bluff overlooking the mouth of White Canyon and the Colorado River. Built by the Anasazi Indians and abandoned before A.D. 1300, the building, measuring 15 by 22 feet and 12 feet high, probably consisted of two stories. During the gold rush this ancient building was called "Fort Moqui" (See No. 37).

If one were floating down the river, Fort Moqui presented a striking appearance. It was visible for nearly half a mile. From a distance, the plumb line of the building seemed to be remarkably true. In contrast to so many canyon country prehistoric structures, which were build in obscure places, this one stood out in the open on a bold headland, and its interesting skyline arrested the attention of river and land travelers. Fort Moqui was a primary tourist attraction in Glen Canyon until it was lost under the waters of Lake Powell. A good many visitors decorated the walls and the rocks nearby

C. GREGORY CRAMPTON

C. GREGORY CRAMPTON

Prehistoric "Fort Moqui," Glen Canyon's first tourist attraction.

W.L. RUSHO

Far left, historian David E. Miller stands by the pioneer cabin at Hite. Left, a busy day at White Canyon, Utah, May, 1963.

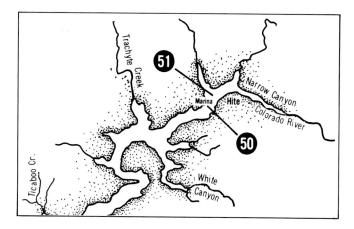

with their names. At one time, while making a detailed examination of the structure, I counted well over 100 names, most of them scratched on the stone walls in small letters.

Members of the Powell expeditions, 1869-1872, were the first to visit and describe Fort Moqui. In 1889, and again in 1897, engineer Robert B. Stanton visited the structure and convinced himself that Fort Moqui was indeed a fort, which is problematical.

50 Crescent City

During his railroad survey Robert B. Stanton came across this miners' camp on the right bank just downstream from the mouth of Crescent Creek, now North Wash. Looking at the accompanying photo, a friend of mine said, "That looks like the real Old West to me." At least seven men—two on horseback, one leaning on a rifle—gather around the good tight cabin and a ramada, two tents in background, covered wagon, pick, shovels, and gold pan on the ground. Seventy-five years later as the rising waters of Lake Powell reached the site, the chimney was still standing.

51 North Wash

North Wash, the main western gateway to Upper Glen Canyon and Lake Powell, was first known as Crescent Creek. Save for the lower few miles, Utah State Highway 95 traverses the entire canyon of North Wash, one of the more beautiful sections of that highway.

At the mouth of North Wash, in June, 1872, members of the second Powell expedition caulked and repaired the *Canonita*, a boat cached the year before at the mouth of the Dirty Devil River. The event is memorable since Jack Hillers, renowned photographer for Powell and the later U.S. Geological Survey, captured the action with his camera, taking one of the earliest photographs ever made in Glen Canyon.

F.A. NIMS/ENGINEERING SOCIETIES LIBRARY, NEW YORK

JACK HILLERS/NATIONAL ARCHIVES

Sunday in the mines, Crescent City, the "real West" in Glen Canyon, 1889.

C. GREGORY CRAMPTON

Far left, a Jack Hillers photograph of members of the second Powell expedition at North Wash, 1872. Left, the butte, appearing in the background of Hillers' photograph, as it appears from Lake Powell today.

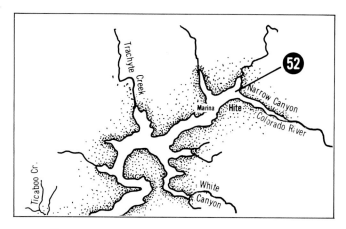

52 The Dirty Devil River/ Narrow and Cataract Canyons

The Dirty Devil River is one of the longest and most interesting tributaries of the Colorado within the Lake Powell area. Heading at Fish Lake and environs, it breaches the Waterpocket Fold at Capitol Reef and at Hanksville picks up the Muddy River, which heads on the Wasatch Plateau and bisects the southern part of the San Rafael Swell. Then it drops into a sinuous canyon to reach the Colorado. Above the Muddy it is called the Fremont, below, the Dirty Devil.

The first Powell expedition camped at the river's mouth on July 28, 1869, at a time when it was carrying a rich body of soupy, muddy, and smelly water—a runoff from a summer shower somewhere on the drainage above. Much of the basin is open desert and bare rock, and summer rains may fill the stream with silt so thick it looks like liquid mud. Jack Sumner, of the Powell group, took credit for naming the stream the Dirty Devil, for which he begged the Devil's pardon.

The mouth of the Dirty Devil, 169.5 miles above Lee's Ferry, is the upper limit of Glen Canyon as defined by the Powell expedition. Above Glen is Narrow Canyon, and then Cataract Canyon which heads at the confluence of the Colorado and Green rivers. The distance from the Dirty Devil to the confluence is 47 miles. All but about 15 miles of that distance is covered by Lake Powell. The historical character of these canyons differs from that of Glen Canyon. Most historical sites and places are reminiscent of travelers "passing through." Prehistoric sites are few. There was little mining, no settlement, and only one cross-canyon trail.

The last photograph in this chapter was taken from the center of the bridge on Utah Highway 95, spanning Lake Powell just above the bay covering the mouth of the Dirty Devil. Dedicated in 1966, the building of the bridge was the last chapter in the history of transcanyon communication, a history in which Glen Canyon residents Cass Hite and Arthur L. Chaffin, are principals. The depth of Lake Powell at the bridge is 240 feet.

For those who are following their history closely, it should be said in passing that a temporary ferry operated across the rising lake from 1964 to 1966, from the time of the closure of the Hite Ferry to the opening of the bridge on Utah 95 in 1966. The western terminal was near the mouth of North Wash, the eastern terminal near the present Hite Marina. When the pavement was finally completed on U-95 in 1976, the state promptly designated it "Utah's Bicentennial Highway."

C. GREGORY CRAMPTON

Lake Powell from the bridge on Utah Highway 95. The bay over the mouth of the Dirty Devil River appears in the distance to the right. A boater is heading downlake for Hite Marina, two miles away.

Along the lower reaches of the San Juan River Canyon.

SAN JUAN RIVER ARM

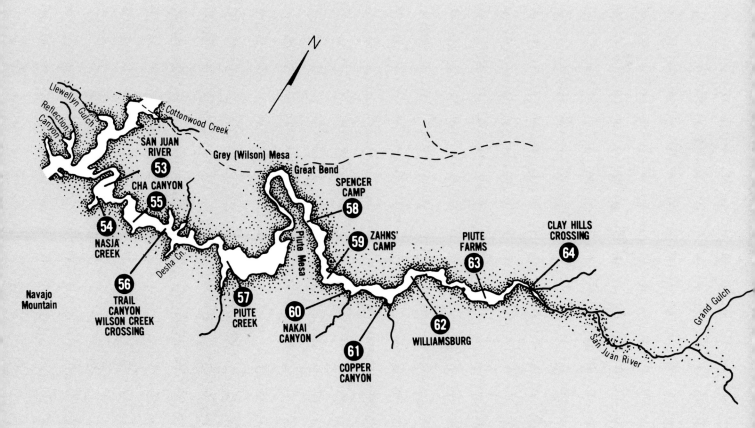

N

Llewellyn Gulch

Reflection Canyon

Cottonwood Creek

SAN JUAN RIVER

Grey (Wilson) Mesa

53

Great Bend

CHA CANYON

SPENCER CAMP

55

58

54

Piute Mesa

59 ZAHNS' CAMP

PIUTE FARMS

CLAY HILLS CROSSING

NASJA CREEK

Desha Cn.

63

64

Navajo Mountain

56

57

60

62

Grand Gulch

TRAIL CANYON WILSON CREEK CROSSING

PIUTE CREEK

NAKAI CANYON

WILLIAMSBURG

San Juan River

61

COPPER CANYON

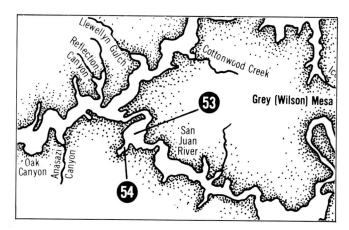

53 San Juan River

The San Juan River, the longest tributary of the Colorado in Glen Canyon, is formed by streams heading in four states: Arizona, New Mexico, Colorado, and Utah. Throughout its course in Utah, the San Juan flows in a westerly direction and at right angles to the north-south trend of a number of structural wrinkles in the earth's crust. By cutting through these formations the river has created a diverse and striking landscape of alternating canyons and open basins. At full pool, Lake Powell reaches nearly to the mouth of Grand Gulch, a distance by river of 70.5 miles. At the mouth of the San Juan River, the lake is 440 feet deep. The San Juan River was steeper than the Colorado in Glen Canyon. Below Grand Gulch, it dropped just over six feet to the mile. The Colorado in Glen fell about two feet to the mile.

54 Nasja Creek

Nasja Creek is named for the Nasja-begay, one of the two Indian guides who led the Cummings-Douglass party to Rainbow Bridge in 1909.

C. GREGORY CRAMPTON

Lunch stop on the beach at the mouth of Nasja Creek.

A research party, floating the San Juan, reaches the Colorado under the high, shallow arch marking the confluence of the two rivers. The high-water mark of Lake Powell is just above the horizontal crevice at the base of the arch on the right.

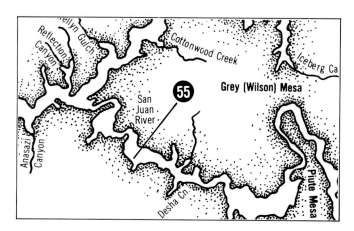

55 Cha (Beaver) Canyon

Cha Canyon opened out on the San Juan River where there were a number of low, flat-topped terraces and even a few acres of nearly flat land. Archeologists from the Museum of Northern Arizona, Flagstaff, found that a colony of Anasazi Indians settled at the mouth of the canyon about A.D. 1100. Being a farming people, they dug ditches, turned water out onto the terraces, irrigated crops, and built stone windbreaks. The Indians labored in the area for about a century, but they had to give up when increasingly arid conditions dried up water supplies and arroyos developed in the creekbed, a condition mirrored elsewhere in the canyon country. After about 1900, a few Navajo and Paiute Indians lived at Beaver Creek at various times.

Thirteen-foot Rapid, just below the mouth of Cha Canyon, was a sharp drop over a boulder-strewn bed. If the river flow was high enough, it offered a fast ride. At lower levels it was usually necessary to line boats along the left side.

FRANK WRIGHT

Navajo hogan near the mouth of Cha Canyon.

Museum of Northern Arizona archeologists line a boat in Thirteen-foot Rapid.

Aerial view of Navajo Mountain, Cha Canyon, and the San Juan River. Anasazi Indians farmed this rugged area along the lower portion of the creek, as well as the alluvial fan, or delta, downstream from the mouth of the creek, where the Indians put about ten acres under cultivation. The rim of Cha Canyon stands an even thousand feet above the San Juan River.

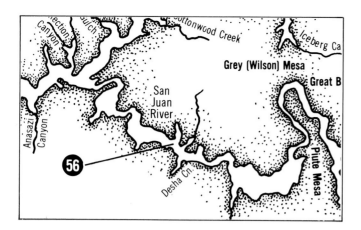

56 Trail Canyon/ Wilson Creek Crossing

This was a major crossing of the San Juan River used by Navajo Indians and by guides and packers. Notable among these were John Wetherill, operating from his home base at Kayenta, and Ezekiel "Zeke" Johnson, first custodian of Natural Bridges National Monument, whose home was Blanding. By means of this cross-canyon route, Navajo Indians used to reach the Hole-in-the-Rock wagon trail on Grey (Wilson) Mesa which they followed to Escalante, or to the Cowles and Hall trading post to trade (See No. 24). During the 1930s the Trail Canyon part of the route was improved as part of a federal government relief project.

Near life-size petroglyph of a horse at the mouth of Trail Canyon.

Boaters approach the mouth of Wilson Canyon on the right bank. Riders on the Trail Canyon-Wilson Creek route forded the river at this point and then ascended the jumble of rocks and ledges to the right.

W.L. RUSHO

Hikers look downstream over Trail Canyon-Wilson Creek crossing of the San Juan River. On the left, or south side of the river, a switchback stock trail dropped down from the rim a thousand feet to reach a small flat, center, just upstream from the mouth of Trail Canyon. Directly across the river from the flat, the trail ascended the steep irregular slopes of Wilson Canyon.

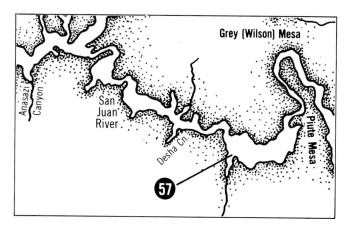

57 Piute (Paiute) Creek

Piute Creek heads on the high plateau country east of Navajo Mountain. In its upper course the creek flows in a deep and narrow canyon which opens out to become a valley nearly half a mile wide at the San Juan River. The bed of Piute Creek, said by archeologists to be easily passable for miles, has long been a Navajo stock route, and before them it was used by prehistoric Indians as a way to the San Juan River. Petroglyphs and dwelling sites of modern Indians were to be seen in a number of places near the mouth of Piute Canyon.

In its lower course below Grand Gulch the San Juan dropped, on the average, just over six feet per mile. There were many quiet stretches interspersed with a few respectable rapids. One of these was just below the mouth of Piute Creek. Here, in a split channel, the river tumbled over a bed of boulders dropping about 20 feet in one mile.

Top, boating party drifts below Piute Rapid on the San Juan. Middle, a group of Navajo hogans near the mouth of Piute Creek. Above, deeply incised petroglyph in Piute Canyon one-half-mile from the San Juan River. Figures are two feet in height.

UTAH STATE HISTORICAL SOCIETY

A movie cameraman catches the action as two boats of a Norman Nevills expedition make a run through Piute Rapid. Starting in the 1930s, Nevills was a pioneer in opening the San Juan and Colorado rivers to recreational boating.

C. GREGORY CRAMPTON

Three photographers hike the open reaches of lower Piute Creek now covered by an embayment of Lake Powell.

113

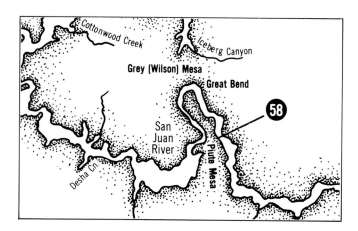

58 Spencer Camp

Spencer Camp, a mining locality, was unique. The gold rush to the San Juan in the 1890s was confined to the river above the Great Bend which wraps around the elongated peninsula of Piute (Paiute) Mesa. Downstream there were few lateral gravel bars, the source of placer gold in San Juan and Glen canyons. But there was little gravel at Spencer Camp. Enter Charles H. Spencer, canyon country mining entrepreneur. Near the turn of the century he had become interested in gold mining along the San Juan. While working at one point he discovered that the Wingate Sandstone carried low values in gold and silver. Since there were unlimited quantities of this "ore" at hand, one of the prominent formations of the canyons, Spencer knew the bonanza was his if somehow the minerals could be extracted from the rock. With backing by Chicago capitalists, he prepared to erect a pilot mill at Spencer Camp where there were vast deposits of shattered Wingate Sandstone at the river's edge.

From the start Spencer faced a big job. The Zahn Brothers had developed a road to their placer camp a few miles upstream (See No. 59). Spencer branched off their road and with a pick-and-shovel gang of Paiute and Navajo Indians, he roughed out a track up over a high shoulder of Piute Mesa and down to Spencer Camp. Spencer named it "Camp Ibex" since, as he said, only a mountain goat would attempt to reach the place. Supplies and equipment came in by ox teams from Flagstaff, Arizona; heavy machinery came down from Mancos, Colorado. Two rock-walled tent houses were put up. A Sampson rock crusher, an Otto gasoline engine, screening and amalgamating machinery, and a steam boiler and pump were put in place. To fire the boiler driftwood was fished from the river. Additional wood was obtained from the top of Piute Mesa where crews felled pinyon and juniper trees and dropped the logs over the edge of a 600-foot cliff where they were picked up by crews below.

Spencer operated his mill intermittently from June 1909 to spring 1910, but the enterprise was a failure. A generous sampling of the Wingate was taken but the assays showed that the experiment wouldn't pay. However, one engineer, representing Spencer's Chicago backers, discovered that the Chinle Formation underlying the Wingate carried better values in gold than the Wingate. So Spencer abandoned Camp Ibex and transferred operations to Lee's Ferry where the Chinle shales are found close to the Colorado River. The remains of Spencer Camp are covered by 180 feet of water. The old Spencer Road rises above the water about a half a mile above the site and may be followed for some distance.

A.H JONES/RUSHO COLLECTION

A five-ox team, center, pulling a load of heavy machinery, and a three-ox team pulling a wagon piled high with supplies and equipment, arrive at Spencer Camp in March of 1909.

River traveler investigates the remains of Spencer's mill.

114

C. GREGORY CRAMPTON

W.L. RUSHO

A.H. JONES/ RUSHO COLLECTION

Top, at the river's edge stand the ghostly walls of Spencer Camp in 1962. Above, Spencer's operation on the San Juan as it appeared in February, 1910. The rock crusher, connected by belts to the engine complex, is partly visible. The tent-covered structure was probably the cook house and mess hall.

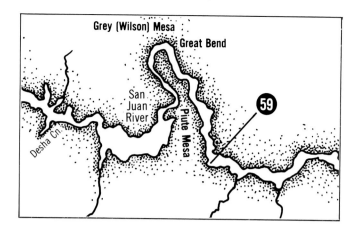

59 Zahns' Camp

Zahns' Camp, in the center of a broad gravel-topped terrace, was one of the earliest areas worked during the San Juan gold rush. Mining location notices date back to 1892. In 1902, Otto J. Zahn of Los Angeles, in association with members of his family, bought the claims here. At one time or another the five Zahn brothers—Oscar, Otto, Paul, Hector, and Oswald—together with their mother, were interested in the property, or at least visited it. Hector and Otto were actively interested in the claim which Otto patented in 1931.

The Zahns worked their mines intermittently until the opening of World War II, and perhaps later. Brothers Hector and Otto Zahn set up extensive sluicing operations at Zahns' Camp and attempted to utilize heavy machinery and equipment already installed on the property. Water for sluicing, as elsewhere along the San Juan, was a problem. To obtain fuel to fire the boiler to produce steam for power, the Zahns stretched a cable across the river to catch driftwood, but it soon broke. During low water in the summer of 1904, the Zahn brothers built a dam across the San Juan and directed the water by ditch to the pump intake. For ten days they were able to pump the entire river up to the placer mines. However, they could not operate for any length of time because the sand in the river water cut the packing in the pumps.

There are no production figures available for the Zahns' Camp diggings. Family members often visited the place, enjoyed a vacation from the big city, and kept up the assessment work. In 1915, all five brothers drove a Franklin automobile to their camp and left a record of the trip.

On the Nakai Grade east of camp the brothers wrecked the transmission of the Franklin. John Wetherill came to the rescue with two teams of horses and pulled the car out to his trading post at Oljeto.

Top, a river traveler examines the steam boiler and other equipment already in place when the Zahn family acquired the mine in 1902. Above, aerial view of the placer diggings at Zahns' Camp. Note the old boiler and the two intake pipes near the water's edge.

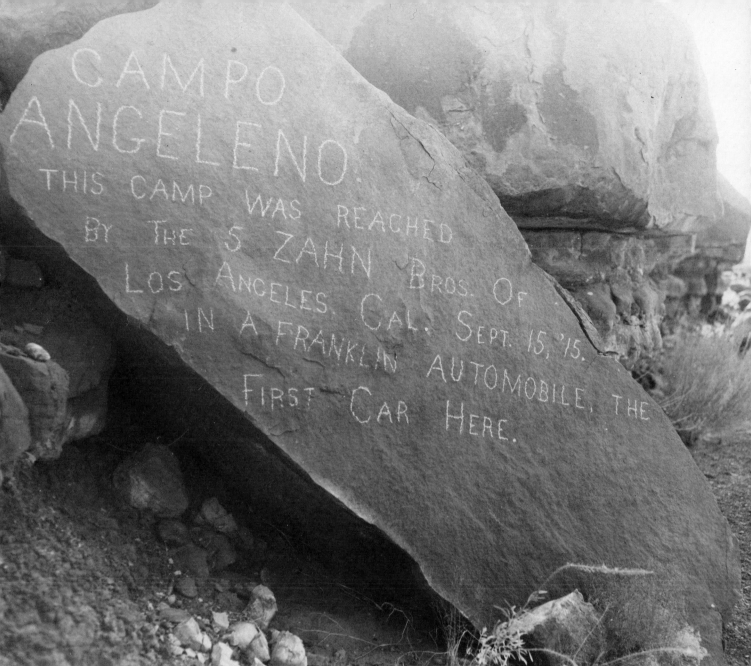

CAMPO
ANGELENO.
THIS CAMP WAS REACHED
BY THE 5 ZAHN BROS. OF
LOS ANGELES. CAL. SEPT. 15, '15.
IN A FRANKLIN AUTOMOBILE, THE
FIRST CAR HERE.

W.L. RUSHO

ZAHN COLLECTION

The Zahn brothers left their names on the rocks in several places near their gold mine. This one describes a 1915 adventure.

The Franklin "camel," as the Zahn brothers called it, broke down coming out of the San Juan Canyon. With more dependable power the car is under way again. That's probably John Wetherill on the front fender. One of the Zahn boys is at the wheel. The photographer's mount stands by.

117

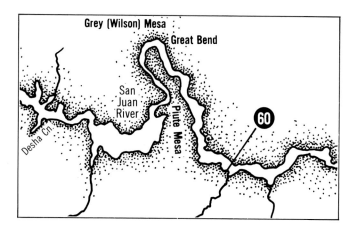

60 Nakai Canyon

Nakai Canyon heads south on the high plateaus astride the Utah–Arizona boundary. It opened out on the San Juan on a scenic bend where the river has cut through the upturned strata of the Nakai Dome. Riders on the trail between Copper Canyon and Zahns' Camp, or Spencer Camp, passed this way, and some of them paused to enjoy the view.

A turn-of-the-century pack train reaches an overlook just above the mouth of Nakai Creek. Downstream the sharply-dipping strata contrasts with the horizontal Piute Mesa in the background.

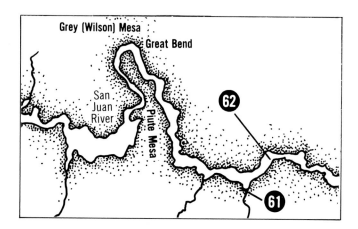

61 Copper Canyon

Copper Canyon heads south on the western and northern slopes of Hoskininni Mesa; it opens out on the San Juan through walls less than a hundred feet high. The name derives from copper deposits along the upper courses of the canyon west of the trading post at Oljeto. It is quite possible these deposits gave rise to the story of the lost Merrick-Mitchell mine which drew prospectors, including Cass Hite, into the area in 1882.

Copper Canyon was one of the main entryways into the San Juan Canyon from the south. Some time during the gold rush a road, in or paralleling the watercourse, was opened between Oljeto and the San Juan, a distance of about 20 miles. Some three miles from the river the road forked, one branch reaching Zahns' and Spencer Camp, the other turning upstream to Williams Bar and Williamsburg.

62 Williamsburg

Williams Bar was named after one Jonathan P. Williams who had prospected in the Navajo Mountain area in 1884 and 1885. On the San Juan River he was trading with the Navajos in 1890, and his name is associated with the opening of the San Juan gold rush in 1892. In 1895, the Williams Mining District was organized at Williamsburg on the left bank one mile upstream from the mouth of Copper Canyon. This place was near the center of Williams Bar, a two-mile-long gravel terrace, one of the most extensive in San Juan Canyon.

Some years before the gates closed on Glen Canyon Dam, in company with some friends, I walked the terrace looking for remains and relics of the mining years. In several places there were prospect pits and open cuts, the usual evidence of placer mining operations. In a watercourse one mile from Copper Canyon were the ruins of a rock house and a rock corral; a short distance away, in the "suburbs," were the foundations of another rock building. This was all that remained of Williamsburg on the San Juan, now buried under 130 feet of water.

BILLIE WILLIAMS YOST

C. GREGORY CRAMPTON

Hikers explore the mouth of Copper Canyon.

The moveable "pumping station" at Williams Bar. Photo taken about 1895.

W.L. RUSHO

Remains of a rock cabin at Williamsburg.

C. GREGORY CRAMPTON

The door was open at Williamsburg's main building.

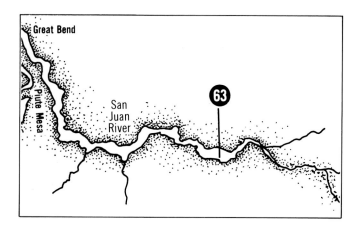

63 Piute (Paiute) Farms

Piute Farms, on the left bank, was a flat, open area a mile long and up to half a mile wide. Much of it had been farmed at one time or another by Indian peoples. This was the largest agricultural area flooded by Lake Powell. It may have been tilled by the old Anasazis to some extent, but in historic times the Paiutes, the first to move into much of the canyon country south of the San Juan River, were the first farmers to locate here. During their wars with the United States, a good many Navajos escaped to the canyon lands where they intermingled with the resident Paiutes and gradually displaced them. Thus, John Wetherill saw Pauites growing corn here in 1906, but when their farms were washed out in the abnormally high water in 1911, the Paiutes left and apparently did not return. Since then Navajo Indians have farmed the area intermittently.

In modern times approximately 150 acres of irrigated ground have been cultivated here. When I visited the site in June, 1962 there were no Indians present, but there were signs of recent occupancy. Six hogans were noted. There was a sweat house and at least eight ramadas, some of them very large. Farming equipment was scattered about. Most of the farming area had been fenced with barbed wire, an uncommon sight in the canyon lands. A main line ditch, over a mile in length, carried water from the San Juan to lateral ditches and on to the fields. The system probably operated on a gravity basis during the high water in May and June, pumping supplied water at other times. I saw no evidence of recent cultivation, but a dozen or more mature fruit trees appeared to be in good condition.

In the entire canyon area, the San Juan reached its greatest width at Piute Farms. At one point the river was well over half a mile wide. At low water, sandbars appeared, and it was often difficult to find enough water to float a boat of even shallow draft.

W.L. RUSHO

At Piute Farms the San Juan was wide and shallow. Here two lightly loaded neoprene rafts are pushed along by boatmen.

Top, history student takes note of the thriving condition of a group of peach trees at Piute Farms. Above, a plow stands unused on the sandy soil.

A Navajo ramada and hogan at Piute Farms. The San Juan River appears in the distance.

123

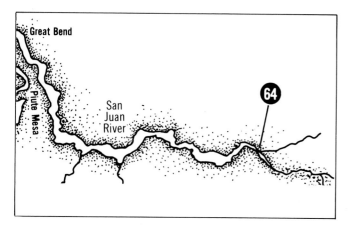

64 Clay Hills Crossing

Clay Hills Crossing was a historic ford on the San Juan River in use from prehistoric times to the advent of Lake Powell. In recorded history the "Navajo Ford" appears in this location on an American map of 1860. During the course of their wars with the United States (1846-1864) the Navajo Indians would have found this a good route to reach the country north of the river, and it would have been a natural route for the Indians to take to reach the Colorado River (via either Red Canyon or White Canyon) and the Henry Mountains, which they reportedly hunted in early days. After 1880, this was an easy way to reach the Hole-in-the-Rock road which the Navajos traveled to trade with the Mormons west of the Colorado.

For the person traveling on horseback or by wagon, the crossing was easily reached. On the north side, for a distance of over a mile, and on the south and east sides, for a distance of over five miles, the San Juan flowed between open banks. The ford was located at 57.7 river miles above the confluence of the San Juan and Colorado rivers. Fording during the spring runoff was not practical. Anyone crossing the river would have to pick the best course over a constantly changing sandy bottom—soft in places, firm in others. Quicksand of the grip-and-hold variety was found in quiet places along the banks and at the mouths of tributary streams. The name derives from the Clay Hills (Red House Cliffs), a massive escarpment towering over two thousand feet above the crossing on the north and west.

The first extensive use of the Clay Hills Crossing by white men came with the San Juan gold rush, 1892-1893. Situated on the north side of the crossing, on a low bluff, was a large monument of stones, believed to be a witness post mentioned in a series of nearly 200 placer mining claims located in the vicinity in 1892. Later claims also refer to a stone monument in this vicinity. Most of the placer mining here, and elsewhere down the river, took place on the south side; most of the prospectors arriving from the north would most likely have used the Clay Hills Crossing.

Once the gold rush was over, tourist guides John Wetherill, operating from his trading post first at Oljeto, and later at Kayenta, and Zeke Johnson, based at Natural Bridges National Monument and at Blanding, used the crossing frequently. During the uranium rush of the 1950's there was much prospecting in the vicinity and some use was made of the crossing.

When it is full at 3700 feet, Lake Powell covers Clay Hills Crossing to a depth of 75 feet. At that level, the lake extends from the crossing 13 miles upstream nearly to the mouth of Grand Gulch. Within that distance the San Juan Canyon contained no known historical sites. Upstream from Lake Powell the San Juan River is traveled today by boating parties who, from Bluff or Mexican Hat, float through miles of spectacular canyon, including the internationally-known Goosenecks of the San Juan. Float parties leave the river via the lake at Clay Hills Crossing.

A visitor at a mining witness monument, looking out over the crossing, is dwarfed by the Clay Hills, also known as the Red House Cliffs.

W.L. RUSHO

A mining witness monument stands on the right bank at the historic Clay Hills Crossing. View is downstream.

W.L. RUSHO

A lone kayak is dwarfed by the river and canyon at Mile 12 above Lee's Ferry.

C. GREGORY CRAMPTON

GLEN CANYON DAM
TO LEE'S FERRY

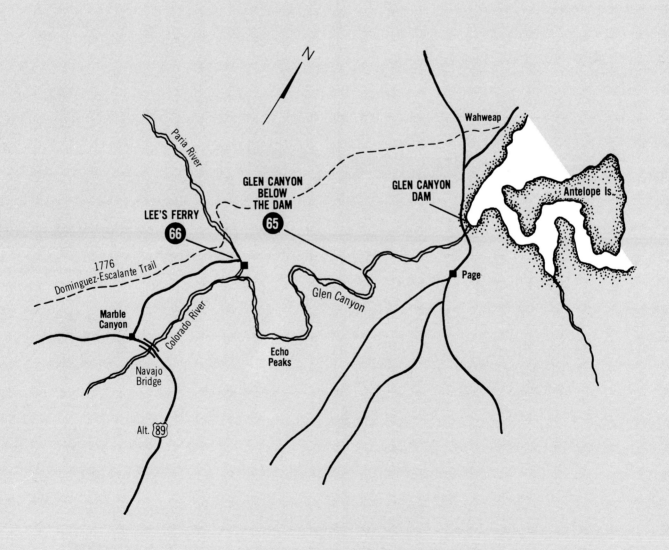

N

Wahweap

Paria River

GLEN CANYON
BELOW
THE DAM
65

GLEN CANYON
DAM

Antelope Is.

LEE'S FERRY
66

1776
Dominguez-Escalante Trail

Page

Glen Canyon

Marble
Canyon

Colorado River

Echo
Peaks

Navajo
Bridge

Alt. 89

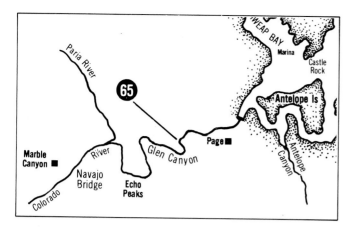

65 Glen Canyon Below the Dam

If you walk out on the highway bridge at the dam and look downstream you see a remnant of Glen Canyon, little changed. Of course, the river is altogether subject to control by man. But you can float the Colorado through the lower 15 miles of the canyon, a supremely beautiful section where the walls rise above the river more than 1800 feet in places. Prehistoric men found their way into the lower Glen and marked their passage with petroglyphs of uncommon style; prospectors and others left their marks as well.

Top, John Hislop was a member of the Robert B. Stanton railroad survey team working in Glen Canyon in 1889. Above, prehistoric petroglyphs in the lower canyon.

C. GREGORY CRAMPT

The towering walls of Glen Canyon below the dam.

A.E. TURNER/BUREAU OF RECLAMATION

*F.G. Faatz made a prospecting run through
Cataract, Narrow, and Glen canyons
in 1892.*

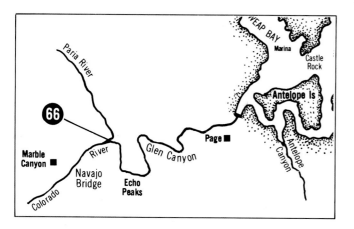

66 Lee's Ferry

Lee's Ferry, the dividing point between the upper and lower basins of the Colorado River, is a place of scenic and historic importance. Here the Colorado leaves narrow, steep-walled Glen Canyon behind as it sweeps out into the open with low banks on either side, half a mile long on the left and two miles on the right. Here the river tumbles over the boulder delta at the mouth of Paria and is then swallowed by Marble Canyon. This was the one place where the Colorado was readily accessible. It was the only place of this kind throughout the entire canyon system of the Colorado below Moab, and below the town of Green River, on the Green, and the foot of Grand Canyon, a distance of over 500 miles.

The recorded history of the Lee's Ferry crossroads begins with the arrival of the Dominguez-Escalante expedition in 1776. On their way to New Mexico, the Spaniards found that the river could not be forded at this point. They went on upstream and found a ford at the Crossing of the Fathers. On his first canyon voyage, John Wesley Powell stopped here briefly in 1869, and in 1871 he ended the first leg of his second expedition here. Before Powell returned in the summer of 1872 to continue his voyage, John D. Lee had arrived.

Lee put up a house near the Paria River, and in January, 1873 he opened a regular ferry service. Thus it began. Under several successive owners Lee's Ferry served as a major crossing of the Colorado until it was replaced in 1929 by Navajo Bridge, built across Marble Canyon six miles downstream.

The ferry business was just one activity at Lee's Ferry. Lee opened trade with the Navajo Indians, who were among the first to ride the ferry. During the gold excitement in Glen Canyon, this was a point of departure for prospectors. The Hoskaninni Company, the gold dredging outfit, set up a headquarters at the ferry. Here, in 1910, Charles H. Spencer arrived to start up an elaborate plant to extract gold from the colorful Chinle shale. Here was the point of beginning for the detailed survey of the Colorado and San Juan rivers undertaken by the U.S. Geological Survey and the Southern California Edison Company.

Interested visitor reads the descriptive plaque at "Lee's Ferry Fort."

This was the main building on the right bank terminus of Lee's Ferry. Only remains of the rock chimney mark the site today. The left bank approach road may be seen across the river. A road from the left bank terminus extends upstream about a mile and a half to Fall Creek. The road, clearly visible from the river, was built by the Hoskaninni Company in 1899.

In modern times Lee's Ferry has become a key point in the growth of recreational boating on the Colorado River. Before the dam most Glen Canyon float trips ended here. Now the river between the dam and Lee's Ferry is open to private boaters, and commercial trips are run between the two points. All Grand Canyon boat trips begin at Lee's Ferry. Since 1963 recreational facilities have been developed and operated by the National Park Service. The agency has sought to maintain the historical integrity of the place.

In a spectacular desert landscape, Lee's Ferry is rich in the visible traces of history. The original ferry site is upstream half a mile from the boat ramp. On the river survey maps published in 1921, mile 0 is fixed at the original ferry site. A few yards upstream from the boat ramp stands "Lee's Ferry Fort," a building dating from 1874. It was built primarily as a trading post, not a fort, and was used in later years as a residence and school. Charles Spencer used it as a mess hall. Until recent years, the remains of the Charles H. Spencer steamboat could be seen on the riverbank near the site of his mining operations. The boat has all but disappeared. Sunk in the silt at the river's edge, the boiler may be seen when the river is low. John D. Lee's ranch, some distance back from the Colorado, has been preserved and incorporated in the recreation area. It is easily visited. The above sites and other places of historic importance are described by W.L. Rusho and C. Gregory Crampton, *Desert River Crossing, Historic Lee's Ferry on the Colorado River* (1981). No commercial facilities exist in the recreation area. These will be found at Marble Canyon on U.S. Highway 89A, at the western approach to Navajo Bridge.

E.C. LARUE/U.S. GEOLOGICAL SURVEY

A.H. JONES/RUSHO COLLECTION

In midstream and heavily loaded, Lee's Ferry, 1910.

C. GREGORY CRAMPTON

The "Charles H. Spencer" as it apeared in 1915. Built at Warm Creek to haul coal down to Lee's Ferry, it required almost all the coal it could carry to power itself back upstream to Warm Creek.

Lee's Ferry Ranch, sometimes called "Lonely Dell." Emma Lee, arriving with her husband in the area in December, 1871, exclaimed, "Oh, what a lonely dell," when she first saw the place.

133

A GLEN CANYON SAMPLER

The rich story of the Glen Canyon country is reflected in many writings by explorers, colonists, prospectors, geologists, archeologists, historians, river runners, and conservationists. Some of the aspects of the human story will be found in this selection of titles most of which may be found located in libraries of goodly size, or by booksellers.

Abbey, Edward, *Desert Solitaire, a Season in the Wilderness* (New York, McGraw-Hill, 1968). One man's love affair with Utah's canyon country.

Baker, Pearl, *Trail on the Water* (Boulder, CO; Pruett Publishing, 1970). A biography of riverman Bert Loper.

Bernheimer, Charles L., *Rainbow Bridge: Circling Navajo Mountain and Exploration in the "Bad Lands" of Southern Utah and Northern Arizona* (New York; Doubleday Page, 1924). The "Cliff Dweller from Manhattan" reports on several expeditions he sponsored to the Glen Canyon country.

Bolton, Herbert E., ed., *Pageant in the Wilderness; the Story of the Escalante Expedition to the Interior Basin, 1776, including the Diary and Itinerary of Father Escalante Translated and Annotated* (Salt Lake City; Utah State Historical Society, 1950). Included with this edition is the beautiful map by Miera in facsimile.

Briggs, Walter, *Without Noise of Arms; the Dominguez-Escalante Search for a Route from Santa Fe to Monterey* (Flagstaff, AZ; Northland Press, 1976). Interpretation based on the Escalante diary. Richly illustrated with paintings by Wilson Hurley.

Chavez, Angelico, trans., and Ted. J. Warner, ed., *The Dominguez-Escalante Journal: their Expedition through Colorado, Utah, Arizona, and New Mexico in 1776* (Provo, UT; Brigham Young University Press, 1976). This edition includes the Spanish version of the diary.

Crampton, C. Gregory, *Standing Up Country, the Canyon Lands of Utah and Arizona* (New York; Alfred A. Knopf, University of Utah Press in association with the Amon Carter Museum of Western Art. Second edition, Gibbs M. Smith, Layton, UT, 1981). The Glen Canyon country in its regional, geographical, and historical setting. Many illustrations and extensive notes and bibliography.

_____, and Dwight L. Smith, eds., *The Hoskaninni Papers; Mining in Glen Canyon, 1897-1902, by Robert B. Stanton*, University of Utah Anthropological Papers 54 (Salt Lake City, UT, 1961). Stanton's personal account of the operations of the company and the building of the dredge.

Darrah, William C., *Powell of the Colorado* (Princeton; Princeton University Press, 1951). Full-length biography based on the sources.

Dellenbaugh, Frederick S., *A Canyon Voyage; the Narrative of the Second Powell Expedition Down the Green-Colorado River from Wyoming, and the Exploration by Land, in the years 1871-1872* (New Haven; Yale University Press, 1926). The first satisfactory account of the second Powell expedition by a member of the party. Contemporary photographs by expedition photographers E.O. Beaman and Jack Hillers.

_____, *The Romance of the Colorado River* (New York and London; G.P. Putnam's Sons, 1902). A very good summary of river history from the Spanish discoveries to the Stanton Railroad survey. Many photographic illustrations.

Dutton, C.E., *Report on the Geology of the High Plateaus of Utah, with Atlas.* U.S. Geographical and Geological Survey of the Rocky Mountain Region (Washington, Government Printing Office, 1880). Classic study of the plateaus bordering the Glen Canyon country in the West.

Fowler, Don D., ed., *"Photographed All the Best Scenery:" Jack Hillers' Diary of the Powell Expeditions, 1871-1875* (Salt Lake City; University of Utah Press, 1971). Starting with Powell, Hillers became one of the great 19th century photographers.

Goldwater, Barry M., *Delightful Journey down the Green & Colorado Rivers* (Tempe, AZ; Arizona Historical Foundation, 1970). A running daily account of a trip from Green River, Utah, to Lake Mead in 1940 with much detail on Rainbow Bridge and Glen Canyon by one of Arizona's best-known native sons.

Grey, Zane, *Tales of Lonely Trails* (New York; Harper, 1922). Grey's non-fiction account of his travels in the West including a trip to Rainbow Bridge.

Gregory, Herbert E., and Raymond C. Moore, *The Kaiparowits Region, A Geographic and Geological Reconnaissance.* U.S. Geological Survey Professional Paper 164 (Washington, Government Printing Office, 1931). This, and other works by Gregory on the Navajo Country (1917), the San Juan Country (1938), and the Paunsaugunt Region (1951), all published by the Geological Survey, are basic books on the Glen Canyon region.

Hunt, Charles B., assisted by Paul Averett and Ralph L. Miller, *Geology and Geography of the Henry Mountains Region, Utah.* U.S. Geological Survey Professional Paper 228 (Washington, Government Printing Office, 1953). A new study of one of the classic areas in geology.

Jennings, Jesse D., *Glen Canyon: a Summary.* University of Utah Anthropological Papers 81 (Salt Lake City, 1966). Summary of the extensive Glen Canyon salvage operations by the University of Utah and the Museum of Northern Arizona.

Kluckhohn, Clyde, *To the Foot of the Rainbow: A Tale of Twenty-five Hundred Miles of Wandering on Horseback through the Southwest Enchanted Land* (New York, London; Century Company, 1927). Later distinguished student of the Navajo Indians visits Rainbow Bridge.

_____, and Dorothea Leighton, *The Navaho* (Cambridge; Harvard University Press, 1958). Comprehensive view of Navajo life and culture.

Kolb, E.L., *Through the Grand Canyon from Wyoming to Mexico* (New York; Macmillan, 1914). Frequent reprints. Ellsworth and Emery Kolb ran the rivers, 1911-1912, making movies.

Lister, Robert H., and Florence C. Lister, *Those Who Came Before: Southwestern Archeology in the National Park System* (Tucson; University of Arizona Press, 1983). Glen Canyon prehistory in regional perspective.

Miller, David E., *Hole-in-the-Rock: an Epic in the Colonization of the Great American West* (Salt Lake City; University of Utah Press, 1966). First edition, 1959. A scholarly, readable account of this incredible story.

Peterson, Charles S., *Take Up Your Mission: Mormon Colonization along the Little Colorado River 1870-1890* (Tucson; University of Arizona Press, 1973). Very readable, scholarly study of the advance of the Mormon frontier through southern Utah to northern Arizona.

Powell, John Wesley, *Canyons of the Colorado* (Meadville, PA; Flood and Vincent, 1895). A revision of Powell's 1875 report with much additional material and illustrations. There have been modern reprints.

_____, *Exploration of the Colorado River of the West and its Tributaries Explored in 1869, 1870, 1871 and 1872 under the Direction of the Smithsonian Institution* (Washington, Government Printing Office, 1875). A basic document of Colorado River history, the book is a curious composite report of the two Powell river trips.

Rusho, W.L., ed., *Everett Ruess, a Vagabond for Beauty* (Salt Lake City; Gibbs M. Smith, 1983). The full story of the life and disappearance of Ruess.

_____, and C. Gregory Crampton *Lee's Ferry -- Desert River Crossing* (Salt Lake City; Cricket Productions, 1992). Lee's Ferry in its regional setting. Detailed description of historical sites, extensive bibliography and illustrations.

Stanton, Robert B., *Down the Colorado, Edited with an Introduction by Dwight L. Smith* (Norman; University of Oklahoma Press, 1965). Stanton's own summary account of the railroad survey through the canyons, 1889-1890.

U.S. National Park Service, *A Survey of the Recreational Resources of the Colorado River Basin* (Washington, Government Printing Office, 1950). The potential for recreation in the Glen Canyon region is described in a chapter in this unusual book.

Utah State Historical Society, "The Exploration of the Colorado River in 1869, and of the Colorado River and the High Plateaus in 1871-72," in *Utah Historical Quarterly*, vols. 15-17 (1947-1949). Diaries and first-hand accounts of the first and second Powell expeditions.

_____, Special Issue on the Colorado River of the West. Articles by specialists on Indian peoples, Powell, Reclamation, Stanton, River Runners, and History in Glen Canyon, in *Utah Historical Quarterly*, vol. 28 (July, 1960).

INDEX OF PROPER NAMES

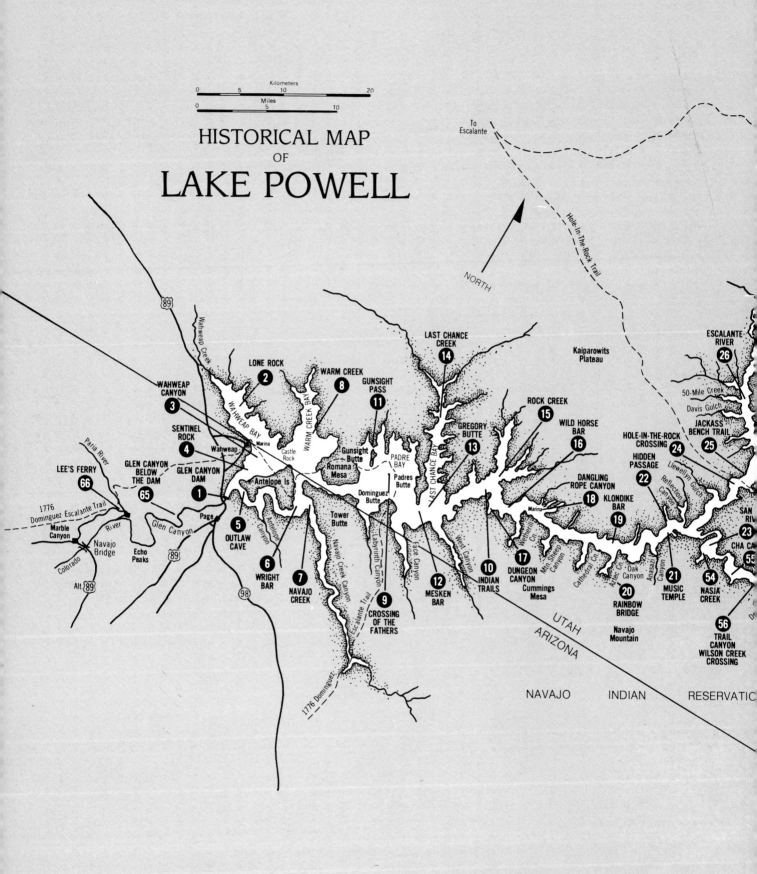

HISTORICAL MAP
OF
LAKE POWELL

Kilometers
0   5   10   20

Miles
0   5   10

To Escalante

NORTH

Hole-In-The-Rock Trail

Wahweap Creek

LAST CHANCE CREEK
14

Kaiparowits Plateau

ESCALANTE RIVER
26

LONE ROCK
2

WARM CREEK
8

GUNSIGHT PASS
11

50-Mile Creek

Davis Gulch

WAHWEAP CANYON
3

WARM CREEK BAY

ROCK CREEK
15

WILD HORSE BAR
16

HOLE-IN-THE-ROCK CROSSING
24

JACKASS BENCH TRAIL
25

GREGORY BUTTE
13

WAHWEAP BAY

Marina

Castle Rock

HIDDEN PASSAGE
22

SENTINEL ROCK
4

Wahweap

Gunsight Butte

PADRE BAY

DANGLING ROPE CANYON
18

Reflection Canyon

Llewellyn Gulch

Paria River

Romana Mesa

Padres Butte

Antelope Is

LEE'S FERRY
66

GLEN CANYON BELOW THE DAM
65

GLEN CANYON DAM
1

Dominguez Butte

Marina

KLONDIKE BAR
19

SAN RIV
23

1776 Dominguez Escalante Trail

Page

Echo Peaks

Glen Canyon

Antelope Canyon

Tower Butte

Labyrinth Canyon

West Canyon

Face Canyon

LAST CHANCE BAY

Cathedral Cn.

Aztec Cn.

Oak Canyon

Anasazi Canyon

CHA CA
55

Marble Canyon

Navajo Bridge

Colorado River

OUTLAW CAVE
5

WRIGHT BAR
6

NAVAJO CREEK
7

Navajo Creek Canyon

Escalante Trail

MESKEN BAR
12

INDIAN TRAILS
10

DUNGEON CANYON
17

Wetherill Cn.

Mtn Sheep Canyon

Cummings Mesa

MUSIC TEMPLE
21

NASJA CREEK
54

Alt. 89

CROSSING OF THE FATHERS
9

RAINBOW BRIDGE
20

Navajo Mountain

TRAIL CANYON WILSON CREEK CROSSING
56

UTAH
ARIZONA

NAVAJO   INDIAN   RESERVATIO